THE DOG'S NOT LAUGHING
POEMS 1966-1998

JIM GREENHALF

REDBECK PRESS
1999

Other books by the author:
Porkfat's Complaint and Other Poems (1972)
Winter (1978)
Battles (1980)
Out of Passion with the Times (1994)
Salt & Silver (1997)

To Anthony O'Callaghan,
friend, critic, and faith-healer to this body of work;
to Angela, his wife;
and to Mrs Margaret O'Callaghan, Roisin, and Patricia,
for their friendship, cheerfulness, and interest.

In finding their truths lives vary in daring:
Worms come through holes and bold men on parabolas.
Andrei Voznesensky, *Parabolic Ballad*

The Dog's Not Laughing is published by Redbeck Press,
24 Aireville Road, Frizinghall, Bradford BD9 4HH.

Design and print by Hart & Clough Ltd., Summerville Road,
Bradford BD7 1PZ.
Typesetting by Highlight Type Bureau Ltd, Bradford BD8 7BY

Copyright © Jim Greenhalf 1999

The Dog's Not Laughing
ISBN 0 946980 71 3

Special thanks to Professor David Rhodes for his generous sponsorship and
thanks to Bradford Council's Library Service for their support.

Redbeck Press acknowledges financial assistance from Yorkshire &
Humberside Arts.

Cover photograph courtesy of the *Telegraph & Argus* (Bradford)

ACKNOWLEDGEMENTS

Some of these poems were previously published in *Porkfat's Complaint and
Other Poems* (1972); *Winter* (1978) and *Battles* (1980). *Out of Passion with
the Times* was first published in the *Telegraph & Argus*, Bradford (1989),
and then as an illustrated pamphlet by the Sam Chippindale Foundation in
1994, to coincide with the centenary of the birth of J. B. Priestley. A revised
version was published in the anthology, *Spirit of Bradford* (Redbeck Press)
in 1997.

An Horatian Ode Upon Thatcher's Return From the Falklands was first
published in the *Telegraph & Argus* in 1984. *Four for David Hockney* was
published in the anthology, *Spirit of Bradford* in 1997; *Weekending* in the
anthology, *Contemporary Yorkshire Poetry,* edited by Vernon Scannell
(Yorkshire Arts Association, 1984).

Remembrance Sunday was short-listed for the Alfred Bradley Bursary by the
BBC in 1996; four of the *Ten Poems for Jonathan* first appeared in *After the
Break,* 1998, and *The Omagh Bombing and a Birthday* was published in *The
Interpreter's House,* edited by Merryn Williams, 1999.

CONTENTS   Page

Apple Parable
Autumn
Family Pianos
Geronimo in the Park
The Dog Did Not Reply
In Memory of Sue Beecham
Pulled Muscle
In Memoriam: Lynnda Chapman
Frank Dobbs
Fathers and Sons
Fields of Dreams
Fly
Still Searching for Jerusalem

Dubliners
Pieces for Donegal
Father Kevin
Raising the Titanic
Can You Tell Me the Way to O'Connell Street?
At the Grave of Yeats
Henry in Dublin & Beyond
St Conal's Island
Rathline O' Beirne
History, Philosophy and Italia '90
Hostages
Parable for Would-be Ascetics
Flowers of Ireland
Country Life
Powerscourt in Wicklow
Dark Thoughts
Oscar

History
Amsterdam
Asylum
Café at Night
Sorrow
The Sower

Are You Sitting Comfortably?

The poet's job is to make poetry out of experience, T.S. Eliot said, not meditate poetically on what has happened. We all start off meditating poetically; those for whom the moment which provoked the poetic sensation is more important than the poetry itself rarely do anything else. Poetry which seeks to transform, however, sees all life as a parable, a source of metaphor, linking the personal and the universal. I first tried my hand at this with an invented persona, Porkfat, hoping that through the medium of an alter ego I would be able to turn myself inside-out and objectify my state of excitement and confusion. Learning how to transform private meanings into general ones took me more than twenty years, although the poems in this volume span thirty-two years.

Most writers are familiar with the paradox of being unhappy but simultaneously exhilarated when they hit the keys. In early life a writer should have qualms about this, asking himself if he is covertly or deliberately wrecking relationships to make poetry out of the grief. I thought I was for a long time; but the experience of love after my marriage ended made me realise that despair is no substitute for ordinary human happiness. Moreover, it is not a better stimulant either. The poems about Dublin and Ireland were written during a period of personal happiness; many are simply joyous snapshots. Raising the Titanic – written and revised many times before Dr Robert Ballard located the actual ship in 1985 and James Cameron's box office-breaking movie twelve years later – is an obvious metaphor for political salvation.

History colours the landscape of many of these poems, although my characters are not statesmen but artists of one sort or another. The Dark Satellite, for example, embodies a long and intense preoccupation with Arthur Rimbaud. Letter to W.H. Auden mirrors his own state of the nation Letter to Lord Byron. Love, art and history are connected to the same power point. Van Gogh wrote to his brother Theo that salvation may be found in many ways, including a study of the French Revolution. Art, love and history may each lead to God rather than anguish, alienation, and existential despair. Existentialism which excludes everything but the self is contrary to Blake's vision of the essential holiness of life. Most of my life has been a search for confirmation, affirmation, rather than answers.

The trenches of World War I and death camps of World War II offer plenty of examples of the indomitability of the human spirit. Remembrance Sunday, and Triumph of the Will, however, attempt something more ambitious than the recital of cheering tales in the face of adversity. The first deals with hypocrisy and injustice: the second poem takes issue with Oscar Wilde's proclamation in the preface to The Picture of Dorian Gray, that "No artist has ethical sympathies". The poem was also sparked off by a trip to Berlin in 1991, Ray Müller's 1993 TV documentary The Wonderful, Horrible Life of Leni Riefenstahl, and a U2 concert I saw in Leeds the same year.

Wilde's preface was sent to me by Jonathan Silver, a friend who subsequently died from cancer in September 1997. Art-lover, property-developer, entrepreneur, Silver was an extraordinary man; an individual gifted with the ability to make his life into something akin to art. His life, as much as his death, prompted me to write a sequence of ten poems in the verse style of Porkfat's Complaint.

Jim Greenhalf, December 1998

1. ASSORTED POEMS 1966 – 1984

Lesley Mitchell Day

It was a Lesley Mitchell day, today
The sky was cloaked in grey
As Highams Park air
Rolled this way.
I say I felt the autumn past
Return today
As skies ago I remembered
Moved that way
Oceans grey:
It was a Lesley Mitchell day today.

Art College Woman

Jessica, my Chelsea longlegs,
Lay down your chain with a bag attached
Unzip your dainty petals
And step out of your makeup
Belted and brassiered
By In-thing Dot
Ringing in whatever's in
Your drip-drop pink shoes slinging

Any Saturday
In the Stamford Bridge
On a tea-cake seat
Crossing your legs but leaving the gates unlocked
You left your knees askance
And Sundays
After dinner
Half the nation
Spends the afternoon
Peeking between the shadows of your vodka stockings

Jessica
Leave bearded intellectual Tom from *Where was it?*
Come
Dance a virgin

In the pub
Giggle your dry martini/ vodka hickey
And love-bite the barman to death
Just for japes
Bandy your randy in the Sassoon
And, sister of whiskey,
Pass me a frisky
(But mind the crumbs O yo-yo knickers)
And bounce instead your incrowd bum upon my bed
Then I'll keep time to the chime
Of coke bottles strung by someone
Around your love-bites
With a hash-bag on a sash
Beneath your indiscretion
Flying thigh
And I up your highroad
Jessica.

Prison Farm

human nature
is like a man with a rope round his neck
when
it was pointed out
that down south
a man had been strangled with barbed-wire
he must have been different from the rest
        in some small way
who put barbed laurels round Christ's head
was it people
                who were afraid he was different
from the rest
                in some small way.

For Christine

Keep yourself warm
Pull over your hair
A hood of white fur
Roll down those sleeves
Right: keep yourself
Moving.

Three Echoes

Three echoes superimposed
circling a stone
                    making boring sounds.
Tap
tap! tap! Three stupid hoops
looping memory
                    making boring sounds.
And every thought gets hooped
before it can escape
and looped in boring stupid hoops
bowling downhill
                    into water.
And so I throw stones
idly watch the trite replies.
Echoes circle the stone awhile
then absolute flatness returns.

For David

The keys remain behind the door
the room remains
                    unlocked
you
        inside the windows
have looked out
                    once,
a day when rain was falling outside the
windows of the room where
I was weeping
                    nothing was clear
another day early in the morning
I sat in a forest, on a rock
near a lake
                    where you lived.

I too have looked out
and have seen you.

Facade I

We cannot avoid the past
We cannot escape the consequences
Of history

A red moon

Our Kaiser told us
We should learn to suffer
                              without complaining
Be strong in our grief
Spook! Spook! Friedrich's jibing.

Travelling

Swept or spreadeagled, the tailfeathers in the still cold, black
Tufts of birds fat from pickings of the soft earth –
Berries, bugs, the stringy guts of mice –
Flown southerly from the Pole
Before big king winter blocks the land
That neither plough nor birdbill
Pecks any ice.

                    Yesterday, after I had climbed through it,
                    The window slammed, cracking.
                    Photo of an orange flower
                    All the way from Ivane
                    Depressed in Czechoslovakia.

Norway panned out to a thin dribble.
It was a long haul north.
Don't think of the sea but beautiful drinking water,
Cheap rents, mountains topped
With Walls ice cream,
The flag of cold quarters
                         Shell Mex
                              Gibbs SR
                                   British Petroleum.

I too flew south,
A thousand miles in a trailer loaded with frozen herring.

Left Boatmeadow Wednesday midnight, unloaded Friday afternoon
In Sundsvall, a Swedish town of mink-farming.
From Trondheim by boat to Bergen.

Aboard late Saturday night a Finn, drunk on Pilsner,
Tensed his biceps bidding me measure the might
He insisted would floor Cassius Clay.
Three weeks recuperation in Florida then this sixty-six inch Finn
Was gonna win a million dollars.
I listened to every word he repeated
Then went on deck. I had heard enough
And he, poor fishman, found someone else.
I paid him the respect of not crediting fantasies as lies
As he was weak-armed with a flaccid midriff,
Couldn't kid or even surprise
The kids he said he'd left
His wife and all
                    In Helsinki. This bird left at one for shore.

Amber on charcoal fires, driftwood, boulders.
The face is the earth's in changing period
Which gives men pause,
                    Beguiling these eyes:
Black banks, silver bars, gold as the light sinks
All the way
                    Down, including the ground
You stand on. Frozen over –
Until the gods of sky and river crack the glass
Spreading a tailspan of splinters
Which frees the land –
Life remains Bergen
                    But the birds fly on.

Think of mirrors and you might be wrong.
The concept of the spirit, an imaginary rocky water
If you catch my drift, pervading vast ice plains,
Sometimes thawing, other times freezing
The swift current; deception
Stranding one on the rocky side
Or swept out to sea via rapid water.
Glass reflects single facets
You see what you want to see
According to your lights.

Newest is the oldest kind of deception,
The deceit being that one can become a new man
Other than he who crawled from ship to shore
Restored, revived by fire and water.
Most only scratch old sores, complain, or seek applause.
Why crawl beneath old walls to pray?

                                        Break them.

Ivane

Ivane does not wear her heart upon her sleeve
hard Czech
                    she lets the rain cry
Ivane walks beneath the trees
wishing she could empty her grief as freely
on the face of the earth
                              Listen
you will have opportunity
of wiping tears
                    running down my face;
you will sometimes open your window
so
      for that pleasure.

Lucky Days

My lucky days
Being over
What can I say –
O where are you now –
Winter follows summer
As it must
Dust settles
Terrestrial
Celestial
My lucky days
Being over
What can I say
Will they even notice
My lucky days
Will they remember.

Gulliver

I

For almost forty years
History has been happening elsewhere
While I have grown in no-man's land.
Although distant bombs and gunshots
Have occasionally surprised us
And we have been reminded
What cities look like when they burn
History has left us alone.

Africa, Asia, South America –
They are not my concern.
Photographs of skinny kids
With space helmet heads of bone
In places I do not remember
I do not stare at them and wonder
What if they were me
I think only of home.

I write about my troubles ironically
And, sometimes, wonder does God watch over
The white cliffs and the dales
I work, eat, and go where I please
And, yawning, choose which book
To read myself into peaceful oblivion
I do these things naturally
And, sometimes, say thank you
Thank you for this day
Which I may take for granted
Thank you for leaving me alone
Even in no-man's land.

II

In the centre of myself
Or perhaps somewhere on the periphery
There but for the grace of what
There but for the fact
That no one has considered me
Sufficiently important
To kill or incarcerate
There but for history
I think I may be redeemable.

In Prague they are singing
Songs without words
In England they are singing
Words without meaning.

I have no plans.
Once upon a time the night was my blueprint
And I mapped out a course by the stars
Dead lights in dark tunnels
In no-man's land
In the centre of myself
Is that where I begin?

I would like to say I can't go on
I would like to sleep indefinitely
There is no new day, it is the same one
Circling the sun.

III
Lying on my back
My feet seem a mile away
They are altogether beyond me
My blood slides subterranean plates
Across my own San Andreas fault
Collapse starts within
When I sleep I fall
To climb my mountains
You must dive my depths.

My roots, what of them?
They tie me down invisibly
They are lights on the ground
Where I cannot land
In the centre of myself
Or somewhere on the periphery.

I do not digest experience
It consumes me
With interference from the past –
The junk that litters space –
From its depths or heights signals glitter
Dead stars, lost Mariners.

From a hidden transmitter
We hurt with messages
No one wants to decipher.

Figure in a Landscape

In a small London churchyard
By the side of the Thames at Fulham
Under the plane trees of evening
I sometimes spied an ageless lady.

She wore Italian widow's black
But looked like an English spinster.
Black Madonna with a sinister
Agatha Christie smile

Gliding between tombstones and cobwebs
Like a child-killer.
She shawled herself in shadow
Until the coast cleared of human traffic.

I was afraid, half-fearing
She was mad-lonely
Disquieted by the thought
That this silent apparition in black

Smiled because she saw through me.
She seemed a stranger to the century
With its Moon-shots and gunshots
A refugee from another country

Walled-off from the madness
In a place where peace was tideless.
Like a spider centred in silence
She smiled among the dead

Perhaps plotting the butler's murder
As she broke up bread from a bag
Undertaking a self-appointed duty
To feed the birds discreetly.

Even the Moon is Laughing

The night is a black Cheshire cat
The moon you can see is the grin

The canvas is being cut from the back
Something is tearing to get in

If the circus tent is about to collapse
I should prefer to make my escape

But the lunatic on the flying trapeze
Says I have left it far too late.

An Horatian Ode Upon Thatcher's Return From the Falklands

How like a star she now appears
Descending from the atmosphere
    Our PM is now back
    To put us on the rack.

Despite the vigour of her pace
Her halo seems to be in place
    St Francis bought her that
    But Denis chose the hat.

Throughout three years of restless peace
Tory fortunes did not increase
    The SDP did wrest
    Safe Crosby from her breast.

Burning cities lit up our skies
Unemployment was on the rise
    But through the Falklands War
    She urged her active star.

Galtieri and his minions
Tried to add to their dominions
    Islands they could not win
    By diplomatic means.

To their joy the Argy nation
Soon forgot about inflation
    Mrs Thatcher was accused
    Of applying the same ruse.

Above a disused whaling station
Argy flags warned of invasion
    But Whitehall did not heed
    Until they did the deed.

Carrington resigned in shame
And Nott then tried to do the same
    But he was held in place
    In lieu of more disgrace.

Mrs T announced her intent
In the House at Parliament
    SDP and Labour
    Supplied her with favour.

The Task Force was despatched to sea
That eighteen hundred might be free
    The politics were then
    Obscured by dying men.

Thus into battle went the Fleet
To blow the Argies off their feet
    While round our TV sets
    We watched the Exocets.

We biffed them here, we biffed them there
We biffed those Argies everywhere
    You must not count the cost
    Of all the ships we lost.

SHE nothing common did or mean
When our soldiers took Goose Green
    When we captured Stanley
    HER laurels looked manly.

Honoured were our human losses
With various gongs and crosses
    Our Fleet came limping back
    With tickertape for flak.

After that, with questions starting,
Nott announced he was departing
   Meanwhile the polls did show
   The Tory fortunes grow.

By luck or judgement war had done
What had defied the Mail and Sun
   A billion pounds expense
   Repaired the Tories' fence.

Britannia's rule is now proclaimed
Except by Ireland and the Dane
   Mrs Thatcher marches on
   A Gen'ral Election.

2. From **PORKFAT'S COMPLAINT AND OTHER POEMS**

Picture Porkfat

Porkfat had a father until he was seven.
Porkfat's old mother is still working at Heaven.
Porkfat, with the power to rise like yeast,
felt himself expand like heated glass.

Roll on Porkfat, try again.
Slow to boil but unrepressed,
watch him peel and pare
to the bones' very pink;
sense the tremendous strength
involved in bending two opposite
halves to a whole.

Picture Porkfat,
yearning for grace,
gothic and melancholy
with rain in his face.

Alas Poor Porkfat

Alas poor Porkfat,
motives threw him
into a rash of confusion.
Spies in the dark.

Before the eyes of the world
Porkfat contemplates
life without humour.
To be or not to be
is a bloody stupid question.
Giggling in the stalls

Exit Porkfat in a Russian huff.
Viennese Porkfat is away ten minutes
then comes back; revitalised
he turns on his audience.

By your applause or boos
Porkfat will adjust, perform and act.
He has only himself to lose.

Porkfat Wanted to be Perfect

Porkfat wanted to be perfect.
He could not stomach his mistakes.
As a boy he never learned
to play fathers and mothers,
forgot to make allowances for others.

Obsessed with his complaint
as he gets older,
Porkfat grazes the world
with his cold shoulder;
but against his nature.
Porkfat hates unnatural restraint.

He is unhappy,
he should be bolder
and let that good light shine.

This World is Dead

This world is dead.
Workers of the world it's night;
without eternal consolations
Heaven is black
and Hell is Porkfat,
scared to death of dying.

Gloomily he turned on his friends.
Insignificant Porkfat would not be consoled
for his pains and impossible demands,
his secret expectations,
and refused to make amends.

He should have been taken out
drinking, laughing and singing,
going at women, instead of

brooding and scheming ends.
But so. Those who had helped him grow
were the very first ones to go.

Intolerant Porkfat

Intolerant Porkfat goes on complaining.
He is not honourable. It is raining.
He betrays confidences and friends.
An insomniac day-dreaming,
living inside his head.
Fantasies and dreams come out at night.
Maybe Porkfat is a bat,
hanging on upside down to life.

Scraps of Porkfat orbiting the moon.
He cannot be identified
but all his parts have names,
hundreds of little truths
making thousands of little streams.
Porkfat tries to divine himself
in dreams. Without success.
Earthly Porkfat is in one big mess.

Unworldly Love

Unworldly. Love flowering in stars
that's myth. There is only human love
that grows on earth. What is this
love you say you're after?
Do not blind your heart with stars
or metaphysics. Accept your part.
Porkfat is afraid of laughter.

Human love is watered by the stars
as we wheel in the universe.
Porkfat has great need of human love
but is perverse. The heart is a home
for God, his shape for flame.
Porkfat blossoms with huge feelings
that he strives to name.

Watery love pouring from nebulous planets
wash unhealthy Porkfat the gentile
clean. He is not fit to carry
so much blame across his shoulders.
He was not made to juggle
boulders. Porkfat bears up his pieces,
his precious few scraps of Heaven.

Invisible Porkfat

Invisible Porkfat in search of stars
don't grow glum. Sing alone
of the moon, the absurdity
of melancholies.

Porkfat is a prophet of gloom.
*Love is a sack, do not enter
its condition.* No world
outside for man in the dark.

Contrition! He spat:
*Love should be intelligent and kind,
not flapping and beatings.
So tell me, O Jew, where does
that good light shine? I am sceptical
and ill. My moon reflects a face
and the shadow of a hill.*

*No doubt other times will turn, I fear
too soon. I have felt the edge,
and moons yellow, white and red
have tormented my deepest part.*
Although with vengeance Porkfat hurt his head,
with moonshine did he hurt his heart.

Tears Break Like Glass

Tears break like glass in the night.
Does someone weep? If yes
do not tell him so, he is still unready.

Through his own sad atmosphere
he must come to pass.
If you are willing
to let him escape through your advances,
then you must be his friend
and let him take his chances.

Disperse Mist

Disperse mist. Miasmal Porkfat lift
from the dust. Ill-timed and misbegotten,
groggy with rum ideas he may be,
but there is plenty of business to attend,
besides which Porkfat has money,
a few unfinished relationships,
and the comfort of a religious friend.

Manifold lights pour down on Porkfat's
ungreying head. Half-alight, he has
the slightly spoiled beauty of the day
in which to believe he is not dead.

All is Immaculate

All is immaculate. A fine and tidy pain this
Porkfat. All that is wrong, slightly out of place,
is a strong smell of gas. But nothing
is turned on, not even Porkfat.
Though most of his things have gone,
he is still here in the mass.

Mackerel

Today I did an incurious thing.
Having chopped the heads from two
fresh mackerel
                    and gutted them –
I did that with a kukri –
I never went further
inside those heads
to see how fine
are mackerel cells.

Leonardo Da Vinci
or Michelangelo, with fine knives
would have boned those heads
all morning, made drawings,
cut into the intestines,
boiled them in fluids
out of interest.
I didn't.
I discarded them efficiently,
like a busy housewife.

Hamlet

The moon shows up
a fool at dusk,
wrapped in something
on a castle wall.

He has time and leisure enough,
the length of days
and the darkness of night;
but for all that
the man is a fool,
aloof, contemplating
his measure of pain
God-allotted or not,
hot on betrayal.

Unwilling to soil himself
in the sordid techniques of survival,
he does quite well.

These Last Months...

These last months, weeks, so friends have told me,
I have dwelt too tightly inside myself
dealt with the world unfairly
been hard of heart. I am sad, they say
I hide among stones. Most of all
they do not like the way I use my mind.

So I await the day when, running through these vanities,
I shall stumble upon the rock of humanity,
when warm red blood shall flow,
putting a natural end to rhyming inanities
and these imitations from the French.
Then, like some raised leper freed from the lazar house of self,
I shall prance and bellow bullishly of pleasures.

Until then I shall busy my head
burying and digging up the dead.
Each poem is a new stone
in the road of death.

Tired I Am...

Tired I am; my head's bin thick of late.
Sing of beautiful things
like the melancholy Jew, the Sun
King or the blonde on the corner
this day I cannot. That heart
means hurt. Lie down and
think, straight. Thereupon

the bed I lay complaining to myself
of love past and gone. Lying there
ridiculous with ill feeling
no good, whatever will, could come from this.

I hear groans and fear
something drifting to a final end.
Life has a tendency to compensate
she said: *You can love so well*
but you can also hate.

Sun-tanned...

Sun-tanned, tawned by the good old sun up there,
bountiful, bright, ever-green with hope
he emerged from the thickets
with a shyish smile,
out of the shade at last;
the light was brim
his whole head sang.

Light as day he flew,
all heaviness gone,
to make amends; was kind,
spoke first, keen to keep conversation
naturally flowing.
For this the whole world loved him.

But then he remembered
a sabre-tooth shrew toying on his bed
as the day, going gold,
filled the air with weight
he could not take.

They found him bushwhacked on a low hill,
hunched and unapproachable
for all his hate.

Through Tourists' Viewfinders

Through tourists' viewfinders the scene is blue.
Midnight. The city rings
magical. An old theatrical backcloth
shows boulevards and trees,
fatal Man in a stove-pipe hat
totting up the lives of kings.

In a silent courtyard a black Cadillac
and a sentry trained to shoot on sight.
Down to the brown Vltava
in Praha, with its Bohemian streets and lights,
we walk back.

The moon above Venezuela
is as red as Coca-Cola.
The moon above Pardubice
is just a Russian satellite.

Facade II

Sunday we slept and argued
And watched TV
We were red in the face all day
We remained unchanged however.

August we ate, made love
And swam in the sea
We were red in the face all month
We remained unchanged however.

This year the weather's been terribly bad
Blood on the mountains
We were red in the face all year
We remain unchanged however.

Two Views of the Sea

The sea is like the human mind
Its waves are dark
It is not kind.
The heart is like the sun above
Warming all the waves
With love.

Whatever secrets break the heart
Sun and sea make bitter.
Nausea comes in waves
And so does love.
Nothing breaks the heart like love,
And nothing makes it better.

3. From WINTER

Penistone Hill

Mist shrouds the hollows
And folds the heights.
Stand on this bald spot
(The wind on the wall
The moss on the stone),
Aware of three trees on a sinking horizon,
Bent on survival,
Keeling against cloud and light.

Here the thorn
The flower and the bell,
The tower
The power,
Tolling cloud and light.

What spring promised and summer denied
Changed between one season and another.
We saw the future – cloudless,
Heard laughter – doubtless,
Felt certain – fearless.
Then winter brought his boxes
And took away my sisters,
My brother.

Charlotte Brontë

What compromise did my sister make.
What friends had she,
Laid waste at thirty.
Three dead in nine months.
What change between
One summer and another.

What company keeps me sane
In the silence of this parsonage.
Household pets, books,
A ticking grandfather clock,

An old man in his dotage
Who will not let me marry.
The gravity of each day
Shrouds the light
That should be my wedding dress.
Curtaining empty rooms,
I hear footsteps
And remember those dead.

But someone must cheer those left;
I must bake and break the bread.
The range: its gates and bars
Black as the heath
We trod together,
My sisters, my brother.
Sad abysmal waste:
A church, a house,
Half an acre of graves.
What can grow in such a place?
Resignation, an old man's necessity.
A flower is not a delicate thing.

Doff Your Cap to Destiny

Doff your cap to destiny or fate
Time weaves the same illusion,
Confused and unconnected,
Turning upside down our little lives
Whose time runs out before we have had time
To redeem the pledges that we made;
Between spring and summer
Hope falls into dream,
Winter blows our promise
To four black corners
And, turning clerk,
Records in leaf
All we have not been.

Night Thoughts

The dead awake
Walking toward us
Their clothes no sound but moving
Out of the dark
Grave figures with sad faces
Walking toward us

The clouds proceed
They have always
Wrapping the world
Shroud on shroud

Has death aged them
Walking toward us
Grave figures with downturned faces
Bringing nothing
As they have always
Walking toward us.

December Song

Who killed the sun
That filled the world with light?
Me, said the heart,
I did it in September
When all falls start.

Who stripped the trees
And swept the leaves from sight?
Me, said the mind,
By poisoning memory
Which makes men blind.

Who stole the bow
Which gave the world hope?
Me, said the eye,
Perspective is my rule
And distance my scope.

Who hurt the wind
And made it sigh and moan?
Me, said the voice,
I had no other choice
For words are my home.

Who brought the cloud
The thunder and the rain?
Me, said thought,
For I am self-taught
And always suffer pain.

Who freed the snow
That lonely winds blow?
Me, said death,
I brought it down to earth
Where all men must go.

What the Reaper Said

Employ each moment
It does not last.
Time weaves a fine illusion,
A seamless cloth
Without colour
Or pattern.
Too far from the past
To remember
The train of events
Which brought you
To this station:
Too far from the future
To look forward
To your destination:
Lost in the present
Forgetting and forgotten,
Each backward dream
And forward hope
Caught in the dust
Of lives
Shuttled away.

Lazarus

Did I depend too much,
Could I suspend
The dust between us
Would I see now
What you saw then.
Shapes disappear
Or drift between.
Did I attend too little
Or too much.

Have I learned or turned
To repeat old mistakes.
Did I depend on you
To see me through
The shifting cloud of dust.
Did I know then
What you know now
Would that have made it clear.
Did you pretend,
Are you pretending now.

Did I love out of fear,
Did I mistake you
Then, am I wiser
Now the dust has settled
And you are clear.
Is this our end
Or mine alone.
If I move the stone will you be there
When I appear.

Doffing, or Getting On

When Adam delved and Eve span
Who was then the gentleman?
In the days when muck meant brass,
When most sheep were working class,

Adam and Eve jumped over the hill
To work down at Thompson's Mill;
There Adam doffed and Eve span,
And Thompson was the gentleman.

Thompson drove about the city,
Bestowing gifts upon the needy,
And soon became a famous man
While Adam doffed and Eve span.

Life was hardy, not that sweet
(Though the sheep had sheep to eat),
Based upon the wool and sack
And the doffing of the cap.

Thompson and his partner died,
And soon the mill was open wide;
So Adam doffed and Eve span,
Until he was the gentleman.

Doffing in both church and bank,
Adam acquired wealth and rank.
Eve went spinning round the town,
With the carriage windows down

Dispensing goodness to the sheep,
Her social round near complete;
Rising above her lower station
By judicious invitation.

Adam thought it wise to mix
With bearded men of politics,
Whose views he longed to represent
In the House at Parliament.

But his road was long and steep,
The way was often blocked by sheep
Who showed no comprehension
Of Adam's high intention.

Employing well known devices,
Adam spoke of future crises
That would surely plague the nation:
Unemployment and inflation,

Rising prices, income tax -
But he did not blame the Blacks,
Thus showing proper interest
In the conscience of the Press.

Renowned for liberal views,
Adam was a natural for the news.
Education should not be classed
On wealth and rank as in the past!

But, as we know, he was no fool:
Both children went to public school.
Adam practised what he preached,
Unless it caused a party breach,

For Adam was a gentleman,
As long as others doffed and span.
Adam knew that human-kind,
Being far from perfect, was inclined

To interpret wrong and right
In a very personal light,
And proved he was no hypocrite
By simply living up to it -

Not through malice, not through spite,
But confusion of left and right.
He could not tell his hands apart,
But when he died they crossed his heart

To show he was an honest man,
Who did not end as he began.
Doffing thus for God did he
Rise towards Eternity,

Bequeathing us his worthy name,
And that of Eve his lady dame.
Nothing in this world will matter,
Providing you know whom to flatter.

4. From **BATTLES**

Battles (I)

The illusion of substantiality
Satisfies the momentary mind:
Monuments of antiquity
Pile the celestial Appian Way,
All its power and its glory
Hung with Crucifixion light
While triumphal bugles bray.
The sky was my boyhood history book:
Towers, palaces and temples
Shapes imagination wrought for play
Among numberless armies
Contending for the heights.
The sky was Lake Thrasmene,
Little Big Horn, my Wounded Knee.
Cowboys, Romans and Indians
Slaughtered fears; my enemies
Went down in thousands,
But millions more appeared.
I moved armies vaster than Napoleon's
Across the Vistula,
Kept them captained and supplied
Against Hannibal and Attila,
Deployed them cunningly,
Countering every ambush in advance
Devious fate might prepare.
Each soldier wore a cross in red;
I played the part of Lion Heart
And, such is the mind,
Reconciled a taste for blood
With God's greater glory.
But no one died in my games,
Resurrection was necessary,
A hand's touch gave life again:
There was no such thing as death.
Those brilliant cohorts in the sun,
The unbreakable lines of infantry,
Protected my timeless kingdom.
History was life eternal;

Even the clouds would last,
In my scheme of things
The smoke of every battle
Rolled round the sky forever.
Blue was not false to me.

Battles (II)

Past the Flying Dutchman
And the Perseverance,
Where the Blue Moon lights up
The curry house and corner shop,
Men and women in unmarked cars
Observe the passing whores.

Singly or in small bands,
From ten o'clock or half-past
On St Paul's Road, Church Street,
Laying on of hands: five pounds
In no-man's land where houses stood
Front to front and front to back.

Strained eyes
Staring into fog and smoke:
Look for Heaven you'll find Helen
Disco-dancing at the Bali Hai.
Dim figures in failing light,
Stiletto heels and bayonet toes
Jab and hammer.
At best some loveless limbo
Where money will buy you Joyce.

Up the hill past the war memorial,
The blackened Victoria banked
By ranks of flowers in spring.
Summer evenings in Paradise,
Opposite the mortuary in Wilton Street.
Food fit for poetry in the Omar Khayam,
Two flights up looking down the street.
Autumn mornings in the Olympus
Staring into a frothing cup.
Brimming over in the basement

Of the Taj Mahal, the very dead of winter.
At Market Street the smell of blood.

Sheets of wool hung from the Cathedral's tower
Absorbed the Royalist ball and shot.
Hopes rose as the King's men fell;
They fled to Leeds pursued on foot,
But soon returned.
The sheets were hung again to no avail.
Marksmen behind the guns shot through the cords,
And down they plunged.

The sun fills warehouses
Long since empty,
Spilling its golden heap of seed,
Filling broken windows with images,
Dreams and hopes long-since dead.
For each victory many defeats.
Streets of stone stained with tears,
Thwarted love, unrealised hope.
Rain-washed paving, sinking setts,
Streets that never knew me,
Neither hands to touch nor eyes to see.

In the sombre alleys of the Somme
Resounding, confounding
Two thousand men in half-an-hour.
The Bradford Pals are
Done done done.
Dim figures in failing light,
Tongues lolling,
No prayers, no words, no laying on,
But jab and hammer.

Clouds shift and shadows change,
The dead follow the dead.

Battles (III)

What did it mean then, that boyhood faith?
It was the sky between the trees,
That slow shaking sound at summer's end
When light is silver before the green
Burns yellow, gold, then bronze.
The world has no end or beginning
Though the sun does its best, rising and setting,
We know the world hurls itself around the sun
And that it is we who rise and set.
What more could it do but reflect
The great deep goodness of a Sunday sky,
The vast seamless purple of Christmas Eve,
When it was easy to believe that love
Was the magic star three wise men followed,
Bringing real gifts to an outcast boy.

Scarborough's rugged clouds
Bore down on us like ruck-sacks.
We trudged a mile along the beach
Between dead sea and spongy rocks;
While the tide shoved ha'pennies,
Half a bus went up the cliff
As the other half came down.
Anne Brontë died here in three days.

Whitby was scudded blue, gull-grey,
Garrisoned by gulls and fishermen.
We stepped down Grape Lane,
Where Captain Cook dropped anchor,
Into the town's salty heart.
Gable ends and tiled roofs;
The quayside ringing with birds
Erased the candy-floss and postcards,
The bored girls and restless boys
Moored listlessly by the pubs.
We at least had something to say,
The very air induced that happiness
Home, love or a tale can give.
The sun skittled clouds to the west,
Bowling rose, white, pineapple, blue
In a hard-faced Northern sky.

And on the jetty, walking out to sea,
The story was told of how, at twenty-three,
I met a girl ten years younger,
Loved her and lost her.

A July evening and a broken coast;
Behind slate rooftops
A sunset red;
Coalsmoke from chimneys
Blowing east to west;
Above breakers a Saxon church;
Men in boats fishing,
Beyond them rocks.

Remember the sun that summer by the sea
Time ran aground; that evening
We were overcome and could not speak,
Robbed by beauty of breath;
When I loved you and you,
Remember? What have we come to

A breathless passage. I forget.

I felt that fate was in the sun
That love was in the sea,
That what I loved would always turn
And turn away from me.

If the sea has a motive or a wish
I do not know it:
I hear it never stop moving,

Making its sorties, taking its toll;
Backwards and forwards
The bell and the buoy

And the fishing boat rock,
Wiping out patterns
I thought laid down.

Tongue in Check

What sort of attitude ought one take
About the new Zimbabwe state?
What sort of thing would be chic to say
In mixed company of Blacks and Gay?

What kind of stance on Cyrus Vance?
Abortion? Inflation? The latest dance?
What shall I do, what news relate,
Not to be mundane or second-rate?

I must have a point, I must have a view,
And, hopefully, believe it too.
The world rolls round from day to day;
But what on earth have I got to say?

Simply being here is not the thing
And, since I cannot dance or sing,
I must create by speaking out.
Trouble is, what about?

Riposte

To *tell you the truth about love,* My Dear,
    Would surely make you repine.
You must be feeling a little bit queer
    Or perhaps you're out of your mind.

Few of us can stomach the truth, My Dear,
    Most of us honestly lie;
We give it attributes, an eye and an ear,
    That we blindly and deafly defy.

Love's not a great sickness of soul, My Dear,
    It's more like a cold in the nose.
Love's not romantic at all, I fear,
    Especially without any clothes.

Love is a flawed grubby boy, My Dear,
    Never on time for his tea;
A man without money, reeking of beer,
    His underpants yellow with pee.

It's knowing you're not alone, My Dear,
    But wishing perhaps you were;
Wanting what's far instead of what's near,
    He's never him, nor she her.

It means putting up with a lot, My Dear,
    Then putting up with some more.
Evasive, elusive, rarely clear,
    Not subject to truth or to law.

It's the cold we cannot cure, My Dear,
    The itch in erogenous zones.
Love is simply the cross that we bear,
    The price of not living alone.

The stars that wink in the night, My Dear,
    The sun that blinks on the sea,
Have nothing at all to do with love:
    They are much better off than we.

Love is a kind of deceit, My Dear,
    Essential for passing the time;
Without it we'd all be bored or weird,
    And probably not very kind.

It's the crock at the end of the bow, My Dear,
    The toe at the end of your boot;
It's the lash on your eye, the wax in your ear,
    The nail in both hand and foot.

Love may be happy or sad, My Dear,
    It depends on personal taste.
Absolute love is a myth down here,
    And truth a matter of faith.

Evening in the Park

Something rummages the Benson & Hedges
Boxes in the litter
Sorting leaves, sifting rubbish,
Riffling yews as though they were trees
And not four-masted schooners
Heaving in heavy seas.

A Henry Moore shines whitely in the spray,
Reclining featureless upon a plinth.
Were the metal copper the hatching would be verdigris,
Not blue. It is not genuine.
Even the gallery windows look papered in,
Stuck on to the building.

Gardeners have arranged the plants and flowers;
Their neat arrangements
Like designs on Coronation mugs,
When floral clocks were all the rage.
The background glazing is grey,
Eternity's colour.

An old man pushes a baby carriage;
Eight small wheels leave no track,
Rain has darkened the tarmacadam,
Washing the tracks away.
Insignificant with bits of leaf
A slight puddle photographs movements of the day.

Through a hole in fast-moving cloud
An icy light briefly clarifies the dark,
The old man and the park.
I shred my cigar butt under-foot;
The leaf crumbles like rotten wood,
The wind blows it away.

5. From **EVE OF EASTER**

Requiem

There is no femininity in death.
Sexless in her greenish cotton nightdress,
she lay like a washed-up shell
between crisp blank sheets;
in the manner of a child sleeping.

Until that final afternoon
I had not connected my mother with death,
could not believe she would pass
the way of other men and women.
Death and her were unrelated;
what had she to do with dying?

Death has no grace or finer feeling.
Her mouth gaped like a hole,
she gasped for air.
No romantic sounds of the sea
beguiled our ears,
but the harsh gargle of a bottle emptying.
Her breath, stained with decades of tea,
had a stale medical odour.
Her teeth, upturned in a glass of water,
grimaced like a specimen
at a box of chocolates
she would never eat.

My wife and I stood smartly dressed
either side of the hospital bed,
not knowing what to do or say.
I was hot and bored and wanted to cry,
but sweated and prayed instead.

In the stuffy swarming sunlight
of that July afternoon,
we tried to impress our images
upon her wandering washed-out eyes.
They rolled around like little worlds,
unpeopled, without sun or moon or stars,
as though searching for an exit.

Her hair, combed by nurses,
hung either side of her face
like straightened wire wool.
Her breath rasped on invisible bars
as it tried to escape the defunct engine
which had pumped her through
seventy-four rough years.
Even in death she still laboured;
but her arms, made masculine by work,
had no more power or usefulness.
No more would her hands lift
metal sheets and shopping,
clean the windows and scrub floors:
they had no more strength than a pen.

It was Saturday at the end of July
and I, with all my life and size and strength,
could only wipe her face and stroke her head
and offer water she could not drink.
Knowing she would die at length,
we uttered banalities. She did not reply.
Like specialists we peered at her eyes,
hoping she would acknowledge our fuss;
but she was drugged, scarcely conscious,
with her own private sea to cross.
Her hospital bed was the quay
where we stood impatiently,
helplessly waving goodbye.

Whatever help we hoped to gain
was dying, though we did not know it;
within three months we two were lost.
What the living hope to gain from the dying
was not conferred by her death.
Life was ours and ours was the failure:
this death was hers alone.
She died by herself that night,
we were driving back and almost home.

It was not the manner of her dying
but the manner of her living
I would do well to remember:
the stubborn resolve, the always trying.

It was not the solitary dying
but the endurance in the living.
It was not how much she had to give
but the manner of the giving.

Death ended nothing but the pain,
the volatile uncertainties of suffering.
Pain-killers could not diminish
her wish to walk again.

For seventy-four hard years
she did not give up trying,
until her strength collapsed
and she withdrew from what was dying.

Unconsciousness reclaimed her,
but her memory redeems her;
not in the manner of her dying,
but the manner of her living.

March-April 1983

Duncan Edwards

When I was a boy I had glory in my eyes,
my heart was full of innocence and pain.
I started playing football in the hope that I would rise
and play the greatest football in the game.

I kicked a ball by streetlight and I kicked it in the rain,
I played and practised daily on my own,
and when I could not play it I read about the ones
who had played the greatest football in the game.

> *Duncan Edwards*
> *your name I'm calling*
> *Duncan Edwards*
> *the snow is falling*
> *the sky is black now*
> *the green has darkened*
> *Duncan Edwards*
> *whatever happened?*

I read about a young man who had glory in his eyes,
whose heart was as red as the shirt he wore.
They said he was a hard man, they said that he was fair:
the greatest English prospect since the War.

I never saw him play a match, not even on TV,
just in football books of photographs that I read;
in black and white his greatness I could see,
and his greatness is immortal now he's dead.

> *Duncan Edwards*
> *your name I'm calling*
> *Duncan Edwards*
> *the snow is falling*
> *spirit of England*
> *that fell before me*
> *Duncan Edwards*
> *you had your glory.*

He never earned a fortune nor permed his hair in curls,
he played football like a good man among the bad.
He never messed with whiskey or played around with girls,
perhaps he was the brother I never had.

Now I am a man I've lost the glory in my eyes,
my heart is not so innocent as before;
those black and white football books are lost, I don't know where,
and I don't play or practise football anymore.

> *Duncan Edwards*
> *life is so sordid*
> *Duncan Edwards*
> *the same old stories*
> *why did you leave me*
> *where shall I find you*
> *Duncan Edwards*
> *who can I turn to?*

Spurn Point

It was sombre at the end of October
when we drove a red car to Spurn Point.
I should have known that you would scorn me,
as we rode the shoulder of that deformed limb
to a waste of mud and treacherous sand.
The sea had thrown back its covers,
revealing a disordered bed of debris
which it would later cover up.

That thin questioning peninsula
curved like the wedding day horseshoe
I had hung in our home for good luck.
On one side the North Sea crashed
below wartime defences now fallen.
On the other a grey abeyance
where we walked and watched our footprints
fill slowly with salt water.

O love divine, we both once sang,
never dreaming we had so little time.
The sea paws the beach with its foam;
it breaks like a promise and leaves behind
a rinse of dissolving speech
and things which should not be seen.
It withdraws from what it has touched,
with only a fading stain to signify
the place where love has been.

One in Three

Do not expect too much from marriage,
these days women prefer to be free.
Husbands are hostages to fortune
hunters, ambition, greed,
their wives' need for affection.
Divorce happens to one-in-three.

Fidelity, a friend said, is not important;
these days it is a luxury.
Careers take precedence to home, children;
money can't buy love but pays the bills.
Marriage, like the economy, is in recession.
Bankruptcy happens to one-in-three.

I remember the day we stood at the altar,
the priest spoke of truth and honesty,
he read a poem by Shakespeare
about love which never alters;
but what did Shakespeare know
about the love of one-in-three.

Separating

Now I have taken the paintings off the walls
Three blank pictures remain
With dirt for frames.

Through these windows of white
I see what life was like
Before we came and covered it up.

It had an opaque purity
Which the paintings did not change
With their naïve and innocent themes.

How hollow the room sounds without you
Now the paintings have gone it is strange
With the whiteness shining like stains.

Water and Wine

Why should I adulterate lies with truth
And stand exposed in a world of deceit?
Weeping unheeded like deluded Ruth,
Who pined for home amid alien wheat.

Tell me not of Cana, nor of Love Divine;
Do not speak of Love which never alters.
Shall I deceive myself that water is wine,
And be led out like a lamb to slaughter?

Shall I be true while she is false to me,
And go on being true in spite of proof?
Is that Christian love or sheer stupidity?
Yet even adulterers have their truth,

Although with others they lie and cheat:
It was a whore who washed the Saviour's feet.

Mary Magdalene I

Mary Magdalene, how did you start again
when your master died?
Mary Magdalene, how did you live again
when your master died?

He took you off the street
he made you feel so sweet
you bathed his feet in oil
and then you took your hair
with every ounce of care
you washed away the sin

Mary Magdalene, how did you start again
when your master died?
Mary Magdalene, how did you live again
when your master died?

You watched him die in pain
you saw him born again
into a garden green
he rolled away the stone
though not of flesh and bone
he loved you just the same

Mary Magdalene, how did you start again
when your master died?
Mary Magdalene, how did you live again
when your master died?

The Last Supper

You have not been broken
as this bread is broken,
this broken bread which sustains
suffering.
You think the end has come, the worst is over,
but what is the end of anything
and why are you so sure
only these few crumbs of suffering are yours?
What will you think
when your bitter cup fills once again:
will you deny the experience

or will you drink?
What will you say when the cross is laid upon your shoulder
and the first nail breaks your unbroken skin?
What will you think about the purpose of suffering
when the second nail is hammered in?
Will you lie away the pain,
telling yourself
you have had your fair share of human ruination,
that no more nails can be endured?
Or will you scourge yourself
and crown your suffering with thorns,
then hammer in the third?
You have not been broken as this bread is broken.
It is useless to prepare for the worst
since you do not know what that will be;
for what if the multitude should condemn Barabbas?

Gethsemane

Was it in a garden such as this where it first began?
How like a painting it all is:
these trees simplified by the lack of light,
this grass which signifies the invisible
because it sighs against your feet;
those stars, are they not like the lamps of inns?
They burn as brightly against the dark;
but what do they mean to you, the stranger?
Do the trees, the grass, the wind and the stars
make you feel a part of the picture?
All night you tried to calm the pounding in your heart,
all night laid your palms against your temple
to muffle the sound of hammering.

All night you have felt your isolated fate.
You stand in darkness like a fisherman upon the sea;
the crew are fast asleep, the boat is sinking;
there is nothing you can do but pray,
pray to the darkness which threatens you,
You know that dawn will bring another day,
but never again will you know a night like this.
In the end was it worth it, that nightmarish agony,
was it worth it in the end;
for when they came
were you not greeted with a kiss?

Mary Magdalene II

Your face is not pure.
Every man to whom your body has been sold
has left his marks upon your skin.
Your eyes are not shallow like fresh water;
every sight to which you have borne witness
has buried your light.

Your sins have made you unfathomable to men.
Their kisses have washed over you,
you have anointed them,
they drown in your absolution.
Your nails give pleasure and give pain:
you scourge the backs of those
who crucify themselves upon your body.
Men come to you to be kings.

*So when they continued asking him, he lifted up
himself and said unto them, He that is without sin
among you, let him first cast a stone at her. And again
he stooped down, and wrote on the ground.*

St John, ch 8, v7 and 8

Week Ending

It is Friday night in Bradford
The office girls are open wide
Legless in discos and wine bars
It is time for a bit on the side

They are spending money and laughing
While outside in the cold street
Little Alice plods to the Cathedral
She is eighty and slow on her feet

Her face is bound by a headscarf
She grimaces through rain and mist
Shuffling past the bright wine bars
Alice can't afford to get pissed

She gets her kicks from religion
Methodist, Catholic and Prod
It's not very warm in the churches
But the cold brings her nearer to God

Sheila has not yet seen thirty
But she's fat enough to have had kids
She's a cleaner at Social Security
Five nights a week on the skids

She smiles at girls dolled up brightly
They giggle and laugh at her socks
She wishes she could fit into hipsters
And her hair didn't look like a mop

On corners the newspaper sellers
Are dreaming of spirits and bitter
At seven they pack up their papers
And drift across town like litter

They must have names and addresses
They must have somewhere to go
They must have had other ambitions
Perhaps there is nothing to know

Inside the bright supermarket
The bachelors shop for themselves
They stare at women and children
Between the things on the shelves

At check-outs the shop-girls are hoping
For something better than this
Perhaps tonight at the disco
They'll get something more than a kiss

In Lumb Lane the night shift is forming
Standing on corners in pairs
In short skirts, jeans and leg-warmers
With cold eyes clocking the cars

The sky is dark blue like a sari
But the night is empty of stars
The streetlights mean something to someone
In the valley the red lights of cars

There's a man in the moon, tell the children
There's a man walking round City Hall
Just another week ending in Bradford
With another one waiting to fall.

March 1983

Spleen

I do not know whether to pity or admire
those forced to be philosophical,
who have to convince themselves each day
they are not frightened or shaken
by what life has done to them and what it may.
The older you get the harder it is
to feel sorry for yourself sincerely.
The heaviest load that bends you
grows important as responsibility,
although it makes less sense
as each year adds another shackle
and justice seems allotted at random.
It is not the fear of failure you get used to
but the fear of success. Among those
who fear for their lives and those
who just want to forget,
the intelligent ones avert their eyes.
Others will do your washing and cry,
yet these are the ones you despise.

Job's Lament

Dear God, have I done great wrongs
that you should sift my little dust
and let it drift, so, from your hand?
I built my house against infinity,
you have blown it away like sand;
but for what purpose tormenting me
with trouble and then silence?
Are these afflictions part of a plan
I cannot see but must blindly accept,
or are they specifically aimed at me?
Again, you do not answer.

I know only that I am alone,
earmarked for doom in obscurity,
unable to destroy my belief in you.

Canute

The sea does not respond.
Yanked round the planet by a rock
it cannot master its affairs,
nor order its kingdom.
It is powerless like me,
but with greater power to mock.

The moon is insufficient,
without integral heat or light,
combustion or generation.
Love's symbol of no autonomy
rules each empty night
with the power to deceive

as the stars, like their human
counterparts, wink fools deeper
into the abyss of imagined
happiness: the heart's republic.

Palm Sunday

I

The machinery of night
Has ceased its roar
Silenced by light
Powering plants inside the planet
A glittering star
Glows off-shore
Time is suspended
For an everlasting minute.

II

I ride upon a narrow road
Not a soul I see
But the curlew in the wilderness
Strong and gentle hills
Swaddled in compassionate green
I long for Easter rain
To anoint this isolation
And slant long lash marks
Across my pain.

III

Bitter words and bitter woods
Are burning once again
Old reasons and old hatreds
Aflame with new desires and pains
What was dying is now living
What was dead is born again.

IV

The inevitable Russias of the night
In lakes of ice lie limitless
No little room can forbid asylum
To spirit making eyes and faces bright
The season rolls out borderless.

V

It is the Eve of Easter
The first day is here again
Subversive in its purity
The sun will set but all the night
Waits only to be reprieved
And the world washed clean with light.

VI

Upon the waters of Gethsemane
He faced the danger
Without a pilot for his destiny.

VII

Out of the wilderness upon an ass
He rode like Don Quixote
And with their palms
They applauded him to Calvary.

VIII

Out of the battle they rode
Into the silence of centuries
Anointing defeats with victory
Long after the world has rolled
Up to heaven and down again
And men have put their shoulders
To the cannon wheels
Long after the smoke and flames
These spirits will remain.

Iona

Light of the day
And light of the sea
Be for me Iona
The spirit's sanctuary
May the courage of Columba
Burn inwardly

Be the happiness I cannot acquire
Stubborn as the rocks
With the sea's seasonal persistence
Fearing not surprise attacks
Upon the peace I cannot conquer

Simple as rain upon a window
Sustain against the day the faith of night
Against the threat of murdering hands
Cup this flickering light.

Easter 1984

Terrorised
by the seductions
of this selfish age –
held to ransom
put out to hostage
sedition
blackening our names –
we surrender.

Who has the heart
to stay put?
Everyone runs
out of stations
out of hope or despair
out of reasons.
Everyone running
out of the house
husbands, wives
patience
compassion, each other.
Running out
of themselves
or excuses.
Running after health
has left them.
Running after wealth
or someone else.
Who has the heart
to stay put?

After eighteen years
a woman unties her apron
freeing herself
from the label of wife.
She tells her children
she is starting a new life.
Forget the past
she tells her husband
find another.

So many running out
I am running out of myself
I am a refugee
in my homeland
I am like Poland
my history's altered outline
changing borders
swifter than rivers.
Chameleon survival depends
upon the colour
of the skin
deep within.
I am in two minds
two hearts.
Like Ireland an oddity
a republic
ruled by a monarchy.

The new orthodoxy
is deception.
Do not be fooled
by the times.
I like being faithful
when you tell me
You are mine
I feel free.

On the Backstep of Evening

I
When leaves unroll their green backs
and the jingling of birds
exhorts us to roll up the past
like a carpet, it is time
to plan hopefully for the future
which has already ended.

II
Spring is the time
sceptics come into their own.
Unroll your irony,
fence in your heart

with pointed palings
and if Cupid should attack,
fire the arrows back.
Keep all doors locked
and double-bolted
against the day
of reckoning fast approaching.

III

You have taken away my Sundays
and given me Saturdays in exchange,
turned Mondays into Fridays,
made Thursdays rich and strange.
My Tuesdays seem like Wednesdays,
all this you have arranged,
turning weak days into strong days
with love that does not change.

IV

Aftermath of Ash Wednesday:
again we begin the ascent.
Despite the taste of ashes
I have nothing to repent.
To the past that will betray me,
I kiss it farewell on both cheeks –
one more than Judas.

V

My daughter waits to be born,
impatient for her entry;
she laughs, already a child,
somewhere above my shoulder.
In the dark, off-stage,
I hear mischievous laughter.
Smiling at my fear for her safety,
she plays among starry spaces
weightless and unattached.
Through her unborn future
we make our re-entry.
My heart, as closed as a fist,
opens each finger slowly.

VI

Fear grows in my heart
like a child in the womb.
The cry of another abortion.

Tufts of daffodils
sprout among tussocks,
memorials on graves

of old Lakeland poets,
propellers for the wind to spin,
stars on sticks for a child.

VII

Soon May days will come,
and flowering cherry trees
will quietly explode
in the city's stony centre.
Then white blossoms and pinks
will scatter pretty ashes
on the face of the street,
and the willow will weep.

Archimedes' Principle

When lovers mourn
as though the departed one is dead
they lie in the bath all day,
wallowing in the past.
There is something comforting
in scum –
the Plimsoll Line of love.

Do not overload your love with grief,
chuck it overboard or abandon ship:
you must take each bath as it comes.

On the Road to Shottery

I used to think this place my home
Now I walk where I am not known
Perturbed to find myself alone
On the road to Shottery

Passing the petrol station, the store,
As though I had passed this way before
But will I find an open door
On the road to Shottery

The phrase of some familiar tune
Echoes in an unforgotten room
It is a sullen September afternoon
On the road to Shottery

Strangers wait outside the gate
But most of them have come too late
Am I here by chance or is it fate
On the road to Shottery

I ghost among these ancient streets
Unrecognised by those I meet
A stranger to the self I greet
On the road to Shottery.

Hamlet Sends a Postcard Home

Wish I had a brother
   although better Laertes than none.
      Try talking sense into mother,
         she acts as though she didn't have a son.

My nerves are murder,
   I'm hearing voices,
      this part is such a bitch to play;
         when it isn't farce it's tragedy,
            doesn't seem to be a middle way.

Must dash,
    they'll start without me,
        trouble is I can't stop yawning.
            Love and kisses from your brother,
                rehearsing death this morning.

Apple Parable

Man
at water's edge
drops a pebble
in the sky
an eye opens.

Yearning to escape its centre
a circle explodes
generates a brief horizon
then dissolves.
Last circle of all
is a world.

Adam
apple of God's eye
bites what he cannot eschew
condemned to die
he reflects on damage
fruit and women do.

From its height an apple's fall
inspires Newton to provide
a scientific explanation.
The Eighteenth Century
picks locks
to divine why.
William Blake
mocks the search in verse.
To right the wrong of Adam's curse
men become strangers
and worse.

Einstein
tumbles the combination
steals the formula from the safe
unwittingly creates
a noose for all creation.
One idea lights up the dark
with an incandescent question mark.
Enlightened, now we
know how long the world will burn
but not how long
it will take to grow
another apple tree.

Now our future's bright
with annihilating light.
God's forbidding Word
circles like a satellite
redundant and absurd.
God casts his stone
then searches out
a place He is not known.

Man
disturbing darkness
ponders
at water's edge
off-centre
and alone.

Autumn

September's fled south to a beach in the sun
   Leaving us with the prospect of poppies
To commemorate battles which nobody won

The season of missing persons approaches
   Some love to remember, some hate to forget
What good does it do to live on reproaches

Bitter the tune of the air's intuition
   The faint smell of burning above the cold earth
Love's fall relentlessly follows fruition

Scattered with little worlds boys kick aside
    Pathways are dark with the conquests of summer
Fruit that was fought for is rotten inside.

Family Pianos

Remember post-war winters
and those cold interiors
of front rooms kept special
for Sundays and visitors,
when daughters brought home
US Servicemen from dances
and every family preserved a piano
nobody knew how to play?

Jean, oldest of my two sisters,
tried to escape those winters
through bars of the Moonlight
the Pathétique, the Appassionata,
looking for harmony
she knew was beyond her.
So she reached for glamour
bringing home
Americans in olive green,
permitting them to neck her
on the edge of the sofa.

I loved those courteous men,
swanky uniforms
friends and I had only seen
in imported comics.
I got half-a-dollar,
my first experience of foreign aid,
to beat it to the pictures.
I blazed home beneath Quo Vadis skies
eager to glorify my heroes;
but they had gone,
leaving me at a loss to know
what wrong I had done
to make them go.
Circling the garden
where I built my dens,

beyond consolation
for the loss of men.
My mother, my sisters
standing helplessly by:
what could they say to me?

Half in, half out of shadow,
I stood before our piano,
an acolyte at the altar
inventing harmonies of my own.
What I played required nothing
but a heart that was believing,
even the discords pleased me.

Against damp flowered wallpaper
the piano, the colour of walnut coffins
in George White's window.
My mother paid for each instalment
with elbow grease and discipline.
We thought labour was her forte.
It was tuned by a man on Saturdays,
in those days you could earn a living
tuning pianos nobody knew how to play.
They were as necessary as insurance,
lodgers for whom sacrifices were made.

Jean left home,
taken in by a man
she'd met in movies,
and June met Jim.
The cold front room became my own.
My mother Mansion Housed the piano
until it glowed like a lamp in a window.

The Easter of Martin Luther King's
murder, a policeman called.
Jean would not be coming home again.
Later, I sat in warm London rooms
exquisite with sonatas
my sister
had yearned to play.
I return to that cold room in my mind
where a keyboard waits.

Discords disconcert me now
the instalments have
all been paid.

Geronimo in the Park

Alone by the park's bedded plants,
a build not much bigger than a boy's,
but a face of such age and sorrow.
He cut a strange figure in the rain,
his back turned to Saturday night.
Wearing the same blue trousers
unmarried men always wear.

He clutched his hands behind his back
like Mountbatten or Prince Philip,
and watched by himself as the rain
made massacre among the ranks
of uniform pinks and scarlets.
The Stag at Bay looked petrified,
he did not seem surprised.

He had seen worse things and more
amid high sierras and valleys,
as swearing columns of sweating men
from bog lands and mill towns
painted the landscape red.
He expected no help from life;
exiles do not have allies.

Old men hoping for warmth,
among the back-numbers in libraries.
Sitting alone in the dark stalls
of the Empire before the bell
or national anthem returned them
to their lives. I used to watch them,
wondering if any had home or wife.

Their solitude reminds me of my own.
A thunder cloud gathers its wings,
a bird of ill omen. Geronimo,
if you have emptied yourself of hope

perhaps there is something I can learn
against the day, when I too stand,
estranged and lonely in an alien land.

The Dog Did Not Reply

He carried his age about his middle,
his mother carried the dog.
Ignoring our mute disapproval,
she shunted herself into the carriage
corner and knitted.
Her son, unmarried, slid back the window
and, as though with rod and line,
fished for images with a hand-held
camera. *We're banging on!*
Unable to contain his glee
above the arches of Ribblehead.
As we tunnelled darkness towards Blea
And this is the line they want to close!
he pipped as we split Appleby.
His mother seemed not to hear
and the dog did not reply.
I saw in him a vision of myself
as I might come to be in time:
a lonely overgrown schoolboy
with a passion for dying lines.

In Memory of Sue Beecham

A thousand feet between the scrawl
of scree and the foot of Striding Edge,
I clung to a sloping ledge
though it was easier by far to fall.

The downward fear of death above,
massive bluffs of cloud that blow.
We cling to friendship, rocks and love,
against the thrill of letting go.

Pulled Muscle

I pulled a muscle in the base of my back.
Now I grope for things vertical,
room to room in my flat.

Inexplicable, this pain in the neck.
Neither upright nor prostrate,
I cannot help but genuflect.

Though it goes against the grain
to humbly stare at the floor,
looking upwards causes pain.

Is this how it feels to carry
the world on your shoulders,
or in your belly?

Involuntarily my muscles contract:
homo erectus on his knees,
more like homo sapped.

What's all this posturing about Victorian values?
It wasn't backbone nor superior rectitude
which made our rulers upright,
but corsets pulled much too tight.

Between two sticks an old lady
redistributes her weight, sweating under her coat.
A schoolgirl slips but rises laughing:
walking on ice, to her, is a joke.

Like a Magnox flask of nuclear waste,
I lower myself into hot Radox baths.
I might have to remain immersed
until the Millennium has passed.

Half erect in the doctor's –
her hair is a sunset, fox-fur, copper.
Where does it hurt? She purrs.
Never mind, lay down and show me you care.

I limp into a massage parlour howling.
Where shall I start?
A brunette says, stripping to her lashes.
Without thinking I point to my heart.

The effort required to remain vertical
in a world of horizontals.
Lazarus just picked up his bed and walked.
Jesus, standing straight is the miracle.

In Memoriam: Lynnda Chapman

I saw the sun
with her eyes,
saw her impatient
behind hospital windows,
dying for health and its freedom.
Craving home,
husband and daughter.
Tired
perhaps done in
but for their sakes not dying.

She knew she would never escape.
She had already passed the way of winter,
leaving time and skies and signs.
No longer defined
by life's expectations,
the hard edges
of the working week.
And I, behind my deadline,
did not know until three days later.

We define things by their absence.
We bowed our heads as she left us
the idea of her death
to get used to.
Some could not and cried
as they drove her away for the last time.
Death makes us feel such hypocrites.

Frank Dobbs: 1922-1985

He practised modesty to correct
the vanities of intellect.
Knowing that praise sometimes pretends
judiciously he praised his friends.
What pleasures he possessed
were offered gladly to those able
to do justice to his table.
His mind was absent of the fads
sponsored by television ads.
Disdaining *snack bar wisdom*
for less fashionable moral passion,
he valued decent scholarship and application,
though deep down longed for inspiration.
He rambled through the briars of life
with his uncomplaining wife.
The allotment of his mind disorganised,
but never less than civilised.
Frank distrusted abstract absolutes;
he knew all souls need boots,
a road to walk, a hearth and friends,
and made these means his ends.
He had a redbrick common-sense
but a sensibility almost French.
Impatient, stubborn, but always glad
to report the good in people, not the bad.
He played jazz trumpet at his leisure
but never blew his own for pleasure.
Unwilling to play lip-service to a part,
he tempered judgement with his heart.

Fathers and Sons

He could have been my long-lost father
and I could have been his only son.
Like a paintbrush refracted in water,
he inclined towards the light of the mind
I sought after weekly in his shop.
Among Penguins and Pelicans I found sanctuary
from life's menagerie. His stock,
I liked to think, was selected especially
for me. He knew I'd come most Saturdays
to scan the paperbacks with timeless
Lamp Black covers. Inquiring eyes,
quizzical and amused, watched as I stalked
the array of freshly-printed treasures
I could rarely afford. Tormented
by the ardour that you feel for another
century, minutes turned into hours
as I weighed *Crime and Punishment*
against *Fathers and Sons,* and books
with titles like types of paint: *Chrome
Yellow, The Scarlet and the Black.*
His cardiganed wife was childless,
I decided, as she moved silently
among Viridian, Cobalt, Vermilion,
smiling at her surrogate children.

Both of them have long since gone,
along with Louise and Aylmer Maude,
David Magarshack and Rosemary Edmonds:
translators of classics I lacked at school.
My sanctuary's now an emporium
selling tubs of ghee and bags of rice,
bland economy cans of emulsion,
domestic essentials at cut price.
Turning the pages of those paperbacks
bought all those years ago,
although some of the spines have cracked
and the covers no longer shine as blackly
or snap between finger and thumb,
I remember them and their pleasure
when I chose *Fathers and Sons.*

Fields of Dreams

I
Chaplin was the name,
my school in Folly Lane.
I learned the routine:
pleasing some, placating others.

In black canvas plimsolls I taught myself,
kicking sodden footballs with either foot.
In Sylvia Plath's final winter,
shovelling snow from White Hart Lane.

Instead of a Mitre a tennis ball.
Dribbling the cycle-rutted cinder track,
Tottenham's cloudy marshes
smelling of gas and canals.

The scrubby Rec behind council terraces,
where gypsies tethered tired horses,
my Bernabau, my Maracana
where I nutmegged Spaniards and Brazilians.

The street, municipally floodlit, my Stadium of Light.
The moon a halo above my face.
The wind, plucking the cables of pylons,
playing rhythm or electrified bass.

II
MGM's snarling lion
Paramount's pencil-pointed peak
Columbia's noble lady
Twentieth Century Fox's
five usherettes torches
searching a blueberry-ripple sky.

The need to worry dissipated
as your eyes dilated,
and the uplit hanging waterfall
parted sideways like the Red Sea.
You paid only once, unlike life,
and could stay for as long as you liked.

Fly

I saw a fly in winter,
a curious thing to see,
exiled from its season,
a summer refugee.

Yet there it was
on its trestle of legs
head downwards on my door,
a fly by day quite motionless.

It did not buzz,
though I eyed it with a frown.
It didn't bat a fly-lid,
just hung on upside down.

Damn thing's a born survivor
I thought and turned away.
I forgot its bleak existence
until the other day

I saw it on the window sill,
beside the telephone.
I don't know if the fly got through,
before it died alone.

Still Searching for Jerusalem

I saw the ghost of William Blake
bowed as though beneath a weight,
      below the temple of the clouds
      blowing in wild and ragged shrouds.

The burning bush which Moses saw
when God established Israel's law,
      blazed as though no light was seen
      upon an English mountain green.

One hand gripped a spear that shook,
the other raised a glowing book.
      Behind his head the sun went down
      in darkness, troubled England drowned.

Raging at the dismal sight,
he howled in the unholy night:
      a soul lost in a distant dream,
      still searching for Jerusalem.

7. From **RAISING THE TITANIC**

Dubliners

I

Five men in a car:
it is a Rekord.

Searching for the quay,
McGooghan almost drives us
along the Liverpool-Manchester railway.

After beering up in a dockside pub
we light upon our floating hotel.
Midnight crossing the water.

II

Lager-flushed Nailor
spikes McGooghan's Guinness with gin.
McGooghan tries to seize the duty-frees;
the bottles capsize his Mickey Finn,
staining both trouser-knees
with dark maps of Ireland.

III

A woman whose breasts
blancmange her pink jumper,
flashes quick eyes as she jests
and trades horse-sense about love.
He once spent £50 on me
before I was out of bed.
Seamus, her brother,
his marriage is on the rocks.
She says he lacks the bottle
to ferry himself away from it.
She exits the lounge,
a piece of animal engineering,
with a lucky stud at her rump.

IV

Five men in a boat:
there are only four berths.
Maloney draws lots with Irish pound notes:
he bunks down on the floor.

V

Bathtap toes and beerpump legs,
McGooghan the publican
lowers himself from the top bed.
He drops like sod on a coffin.
As his arse appears,
a porthole in his sky-blue Y-fronts
reveals a big fleshy world,
between two balloons of blue.

VI

Through Dublin's dockland dawn
we drive from the Leinster
in McGooghan's green Rekord.
The radio says Andropov's dead.
Breakfast television shows him
in his salad-dressing of death.
The others disperse to feast.
I pull up the windows to the morning,
overlooking St Stephen's Green.
Smoking above the traffic
I search the horizon's hills,
wondering what love I shall discover.

VII

We enter St James' Gate,
and the world's biggest stout factory.
Our host is Billy Porter:
florid, blond, and quick on his feet.
The difference between anxiety and panic,
he announces. *Anxiety is the first time*
you cannot do it a second time.
Panic is the second time
you cannot do it the first time.

Aidan, his aide-de-camp,
tapers below untidy white hair
like a slight poet.
Picking at his herring
he talks softly about cruelty
to fish. Six years in Guinness:
twenty in tourism:
before that the Press.

Now he is restless.
He leaves half his soup
and most of his dinner,
doesn't attempt the sweet.

Billy Porter scoffs all three courses
and, for a final flourish,
calls for cheese and biscuits.

VIII

Eamonn drives us
round the monuments
in a mini-bus.

By Kilmainham Jail I thought of you,
serving time behind Victoria's bars.
In Phoenix Park I needed you.

IX

Streets broad as rivers,
bar-rooms narrow as the border
on a glass of porter.
A hot port when you're ready!
How about Port Said?
Nesbitt's barman replied,
fetching blood-warm wine
with a quarter of moon in the water.

X

Guinness is good for you –
the old ad is reassuring.
As they say in South Africa,
there is something satisfying
in slowly
        putting away
               the blacks.
This is my body:
black and bitter
with a dog collar of froth.
In Dublin even heretics
believe Guinness is God.

XI

In Dublin only men
pull pints behind bars.
Barmaids are unseemly,
too great a temptation it seems
to barflies guzzling porter
at these jakes.
Would bold Jackeens scream
blue murder to be served by a Gill
behind a counter at Bewley's?
Men's manners are no better in hotels,
yet they are full of girls.
I am interrupted in my room
three times daily by maids.
Is everything all right?
I suppose so, I don't know.

XII

Pillar-boxes are Republican green,
but they spell telephone like Germans.
The Shelbourne was shelled in 1916
when the Easter Rising fell.

XIII

Scruffy supplicant holds a beaten-copper bowl,
kneeling to beg on O'Connell Bridge.
Outside the Anglo-Irish Bank
a woman feeds a baby from a bottle:
she begs without asking.
An urchin in an itchy fawn duffle
crayons pictures in Grafton Street;
Christy, he chalks with his colours.
Down the road a girl, perhaps his sister,
draws pictures like her brother.
He looks up as I look down,
for an instant our eyes meet.
I give him nothing.

XIV

Where Grafton Street and Duke Street meet
gift-wrapped blooms with white-wing collars
power the morning with red and white explosions.

In Moore Street Market
I think of Boris Pasternak,
his hungry unsatisfied love,
his passion for vitality
strength and colour.
I see him startled by the fruit and veg.

From a bookshop I take a handbill,
a poem of his called February
printed over a photograph.
Beneath a flat cap Pasternak,
wrapped in a long black coat,
sits tensely on a garden bench.
It could be Gethsemane in winter.
He stares at the camera
as though it is a gun.

Unfortunately, he looks like E. L. Wisty.

XV
On the roof of the Mary Rose Café
a pink-jumpered man
plays Song to Guy
on a Bechstein Grand.
Moodily mooching the mall,
a brooding youth –
white raincoat with unnecessary accessories –
searches for Oscar Wilde,
or maybe Dorian Gray.

XVI
Saturday morning suitably attired and sober
we go to pay our respects to Trinity College Library.

Upturned dragonship in dry dock
creaking below its rafter of ribs.
Mausoleum of maggoty books,
faggots stacked sideways, tinderwood.

The smell of the crypt
hovers over The Book of Kells,
perfectly preserved under glass
like St Bernadette or Lenin.

Brown linoleum underfoot.
Except for our self-consciously squelching soles,
mummified silence prevails in this Valhalla
patrolled by ancient men with radios.

XVII

Larkin labours on O'Connell Street,
upraised arms supporting
an invisible cornucopia.
Burke reflects on France's Revolution
the lessons Irishmen did not learn.

Parnell, Protestant landlord from Wicklow,
ponders how a nation's fate
guttered on adultery.
The Bank of Ireland
still bears the bullets' stigmata.

XVIII

A church spire:
its sharpened pencil points
to a cross in the sky,
where God is buried.

XIX

City of the Trinity:
Guinness, God and History.

XX

City of light,
and shite and mullions.
Elegant, unsightly
slut in heavenly blue.
Quays of many burdens nightly.

Leafy rustling Dub.
Swift-witted, salty,
mucky as ha'pence. Snugly
bar-lit and star-lit,
fool of eternity.

City of touters,
tripe and visions.
Expansive under flood,
narrow-minded as the border.
Blood-troubled, wake of love.

XXI

Cloistered all afternoon,
painting this portrait in my room.
At seven-thirty McGooghan
comes to take me to Nailor,
Barebones and Maloney.
They're awash in Grafton Street,
having been drinking like sailors
since noon. We look for a place to eat.

Agog at the giggling near a brightly-lit store,
we see a man on the fiddle
and another on guitar.
A youth in a Marx Brothers coat
dances like a moth-eaten bear,
his Homburg too big for Primo Carnera.

Between two architraves a punk,
last of the Mohicans,
skull plumed like a Greek general.
Hanging from his shoulders,
a leopardskin cape roars
to his heels like Victoria Falls.
Cetewayo, white Zulu.

We scoff in Solomon Grundy's,
then go for Guinness to McDaid's.
St Brendan the Behan did his boozing here.
McDaid's, I am told, is hard-line
Republican. *Order a Black and Tan,*
I dare McGooghan. A young curate
insists, in a friendly way,
green raffle tickets might be a good buy.
What's the prize? Tea for two
with Gerry Adams, a Black and Decker
with drills an optional extra?
It's a large toy bear.

Nailor, bolshie when he's had a few,
demands to know the money's destination.
All of us assume the IRA.
It takes a child to America
and pays for an operation.

I return to the Shelbourne,
the others go carousing God knows where.
At midnight Maloney rings from his room:
it is time for serious drinking.

Into the breech of Room 303
Maloney, Nailor and Yours Truly
soldier through a litre of Beefeaters,
Barebones and McGooghan
half as much of whiskey.
Can I just say, no way
am I sleeping in my bed, says Maloney -
Nailor has salted his sheets with nuts.
He blames McGooghan who barks like a seal,
flapping his arms and legs.
Jesus! I need a big woman, he says.
Barebones snaps everybody:
Nailor rags Maloney.
About to assault his McKinley's,
McGooghan regurgitates instead.
He bolts to the bog and locks himself in,
we hear him cackle maniacally.
Something clatters like tin.
Jesus! He's torpedoed the karsi.
Later, oiled and rat-arsed,
he contrives to eject
Barebones, Nailor and Maloney.
They bring up a fire extinguisher,
he gives in, they gain entry.

Before getting loaded in 303,
McGooghan swears he saw Willie John McBride
downstairs in the bar. I confess I missed
Irish rugby's national pride,
but met Hughie Green three times.

XXII

Somehow we slept,
somehow we rise,
somehow we go down,
somehow we eat.

After greasing our stomachs,
McGooghan retreats to mass
while I go to St Stephen's Green,
to keep an appointment
with the ghost of Joyce.

Portrait of the artist as an old man
having trouble with his eyes.
Old hero of mine
smiling quizzically at me.
Words are porters, say the trees.
Only order them
                    whispers Joyce.

Pieces for Donegal

I

Through snow to Stranraer,
St David to Larne.
Crossing Ulster with Van,
Londonderry, Strabane.

Midnight Sunday in Donegal town,
all were dancing or drinking.
Parking down by the river
the cold made us shiver,
we drank it in going to Killian.
Monday morning at Burke's
no thought of work
stopped the crack in the kitchen.
We had breakfast for lunch,
left for Bruckless to crunch
the finicky sand of Fintra.
At the eve of the day
we paced Fintra Bay,
where your daddy played football and tig.

The road was a bender
where the Tans lost a Tender,
and a man once built a bridge.
On Malin Head coast
by the wrecked customs post
Denny sketched the history of Erin,
ambushed with asides
on Gaelic besides
and, almost, The Bonny Shoals of Herring.

The following day,
the sun warm as hay,
we played on headrocks of Muckrass.
A dolphin in motion,
Heaven rolled in the ocean,
on to Carrick, Kilcar and Bunglas.
Its hair full of red,
the sun lowered its head
as we walked the beach at Maghera.
Evening was violet and white,
a prayer in the night,
a circle of light at Adara.
There are nights when I drink
and days when I think
of smoky Blue Stacks at Frosses,
and that dawn by the well,
cold and tired as hell,
when a circle of light
shone above us.

Patrick Kavanagh
Not a man known for the dancing,
not a raconteur to set alight
hearts in chilly hillside kitchens;
the church hall of his soul
long ago deserted.
His mind gave life a dimension
beyond the pale of human settlement.
From the wider circles he banished himself,
choosing solitude's ante-room
to prepare for lonely death
he knew would come to him.

III

Gales mourning lost souls
sculpted the lagoons below Malin Head,
so calm this evening.
Into each cove grief without ceasing
echoes for those who are flying,
and those who have fled
slaughter, famine and vendetta
to the parish of America.
The day's last light burns down,
inflaming the longing to be gone.
This is the last landfall
the sea remembers, each ungrateful edge.

Years of children's respect
made a mark on Denny.
He taught each child to remember,
thinking knowledge property
of a kind neither pillage
nor exile could disinherit.
Water fleshes Five Fingers Strand
more easily than I can strip
history down to its skeleton.
Nor would I be a betting man
in a country hostage to its memory,
where the only sin is forgetting.

IV

Water courses
decrepit horses
steaming in the rain.
Limestone valleys
firedamp alleys
digging foundations
laying tracks for trains.

Navvies' lodgings
landlords dodging
porter, pints of, plain.
Church on Sundays
labour Mondays
six days' creation
on the seventh pain.

Summer lightning
God's finger writing
mapping rough terrain.
From the plough lands
through the proud lands
to the cloud lands
fields of rain.

V

Dust on the fields of Ireland
dust on the green grass of home
dust in Heaven above us
dust burning Hell below.

> *Will you be back tomorrow*
> *Won't you come back tomorrow?*

Dust blown upon the water
dust the coast within your sights
dust in the eye of reason
if there's reason in the lights.

> *Will you be back tomorrow*
> *Won't you come back tomorrow*

Dust the castles that have fallen
dust the houses broken up for stone
dust the wild winter blowing
dust the wild geese have flown.

> *Will you be back tomorrow*
> *Won't you come back tomorrow?*

VI

Out of darkness like a pardon
silence falls across the garden
   for in a sentence anything can hide.
We feel nothing much worth saying,
unaccustomed to prayer or praying,
   as we turn to face the turning of the tide.

Rosy dawns and bloody sunsets,
April's blondes and autumn's brunettes,
    high on Mountain Dew we can't retreat.
Evening's sad sweet voices calling,
dawn's irrational fear of falling,
    the sky's wrapped in the sea below our feet.

There's a halo around the moon
but all thoughts of Clair de Lune
    are banished from the island by the drums.
As that holy circle recedes
storms will shake and snare the reeds,
    and sea fill all the fields as morning comes.

From the border to the coast
those who love and hate the most
    offer up each other in sacrifice.
As they bargain, plot and shatter
love and friendship cease to matter,
    as the sea roars in the rolling of the dice.

VII

Despite a thousand years of Christianity
this is no place for a saviour,
unless Columba catches the midnight ferry.

Like a bullet I ricochet
out of control among the centuries:
everything I hit wounds me.

In a land where death is still
the last refuge of the desperate,
pick any age and it will kill.

Stars are a distant consolation.
The slurry of grudges
nourishes another hunger.
I eat my meal of thorns.

Father Kevin

A thousand years after Columba
    you fly in holding beads
  trading among trials and betrayals,
    dressed in widower's weeds.
Bright as a stained-glass window,
    honesty shines through your skin;
  but most of the natives are sinners,
    and what do you know about sin?

At home you could have been happy
    among turf-cutters and sods;
  over there the cheating is easy,
    the poor can't afford flashy gods.
But the world was aimed at your shoulders,
    and Heaven's an uphill track.
  You chose the road to Golgotha,
    and now there's no turning back.

Far from the hills of Donegal
    the shepherd searches for sheep,
  here the Devil drives friendly bargains
    and goods are abundant and cheap.
Supplied with bread in abundance,
    how many are hungry for grace?
  Father Kevin praying for patience
    wearing a puzzled but earnest face.

Father Kevin among the faithless,
    they are neither false nor true;
  Father Kevin praying for patients,
    does anyone pray for you?
You kneel among the hospital beds
    and offer the bread of Heaven;
  only the dying know what it is to be hungry,
    can you feed them all Father Kevin?

Raising the Titanic

From Queenstown, Cork,
Ulster's great White Star
points proudly towards New York.

It glows like a grand hotel,
dismissing darkness where nightmares
hide fangs among pack ice.

Mesaba warns of gathering packs
of wolfish ice, but sparks
has his head down in the radio shack,

wiring messages from millionaires
to unsuspecting heirs.
The captain rings for more speed.

Californian's telegraphist morses a warning,
then shuts down his Marconi
yawning. Lord, the captain, goes to bed.

Ice clinks into night-caps:
the band plays ragtime:
time enough for one last round,

one last hand before morning.
A moonless mass slices the steel envelope,
like a finger a letter of mourning.

Protestants hammered the steel,
rammed the bolts and did the drilling;
they laid the future in that keel

no Teig had touched. Unbaptised,
the ship they thought unsinkable
slipped backwards to meet the tide.

Titanic was their ark, their covenant:
double-bottomed, more water-tight
than any Home Rule argument.

It sank in less time than the debate.
Like Ireland it broke in two,
leaving corpses for ships that came too late.

Titanic, we were often told,
was perfectly preserved despite
years of darkness and miles of cold;

one day they would raise it,
and we would see it whole.
I wanted to believe that was so.

But only dreams and nightmares last.
What future is possible, I'd like to know,
when the present collides with the past?

Can You Tell Me the Way to O'Connell Street?

I
In Dublin, where chic
women go round in trousers
and men with pale monastic faces
wear ponytails so neat,
I am accosted by an old josser:
Can you tell me the way to O'Connell Street?

II
Solitary tractarian in a sackcloth suit
holds a sign outside Laura Ashley:
Man Shall Give an Account of Himself!
Precisely. A ragged band plays
California Dreaming. The crowd
ignores the man in black,
the sour wine of his grapes of wrath.
In a store-way where the sun never shines
three swigging punks dream
of LA – promised land
of work and money – as the band
storms All Along the Watchtower.

III

A Grafton Street sax
appeals to the plaintive.
In Dublin marriage
always seems a good idea,
yet perfectly impossible.
Irish women will love you,
hearts as big as houses,
till the cows come in;
but prove erratic and aloof
if you require understanding.
I own neither cattle nor roof,
yet I can love in kind.
An Irish heart
and an English mind:
only the accent is fake.

IV

Viridian Liffey in late light,
aquatic meridian
of longings I cannot quell.
The inner man is raving
fit to wake the Millennium.

V

Whelps wet hairless dewlaps,
half-seas over in Davy Byrne's
where Ulysses sipped burgundy
and bedevilled his kidneys
with unsocial gorgonzola.

Iced minerals clink. Where
heated men of letters
sank hot Jamesons,
solicitors now hold court.
Before the Rising,

Joyce, Griffith and Gogarty,
thirsting for news, disputes,
anecdotes, sang and recited poetry
upstairs. Then there was sport
in the Bailey.

The year uncivil war
broke Arthur's heart,
the Devil's heir
disowned the Treaty.
A bullet despatched Collins

and Ireland into the dark.
Lawyers discuss European torts
where Parnell was wont to swallow a few.
They carried him out on a bier.
I'll not go in, though drink tonight is a good idea.

At the Grave of Yeats in Sligo

Well, Wild Bill,
as doubtless prophetic Ezra said,
so this is where they
finally put you down.
A sombre estate in a country
churchyard, half-an-acre
under sycamores and stars.
I expected something less homely,
more Homeric or Wagnerian
for a statesman who won
Nobel's prize for poetry.
I forgot your last injunction:
No marble...limestone
quarried near the spot.
Why would you want
an Assyrian monument
smote from twenty tons
of Derbyshire by Epstein?
You were the Swan of Coole:
no need for a tomb among
the fashionable in Paris.
A simple slab surrounded
by a stone would do.
Austere, one might say
severe with grace;
like a Presbyterian fireplace.
The epitaph's sententious:
Cast a cold eye

On life, on death.
Horseman, pass by.
Wilder for women than Bertie –
he of the rustling hands –
you spent your prize
on monkey glands;
your *cold eye* ironic.
Alas, chilly tourists
pause for snaps,
they do not *pass by.*
Dead poets are such a tonic.

Henry in Dublin & Beyond

Emperor Behan divided the world
into invalids and nurses.
John Berryman, alias Henry Bones,
which one of them were you?

Peering at me from a Dublin bar
more than a quarter of a century ago,
bearded gorgeously like a Sikh,
in thick-framed glasses,

black-coated shoulders hunched
over a golden drop below.
Nervous fingers flared,
bridging the gap, banishing the gulf,

spread to Ahab qualms, stroke
the hand of ignorant argument
or grab it by the throat. Dressed beautifully,
but coming apart at the seams.

Which one would make it:
Henry, with his inspiring jumps,
or crazy perspiring John?
You poured yourself into everything.

The Irish warmed to your treble measures
of intensity, passion and bardic wit.
To the unattached especially
solicitous. Your own hold on happiness

precarious. Certainly odder
than punctilious Frost, more generous.
You found sanctuary beyond the Dodder
with your third and Irish wife,

until your own true country of the dead
called you back to return and die.
You chose a Minneapolis morning
to put Pascal's Wager to the test.

On the Washington Avenue Bridge
he weighed all up. Children, art, fame:
three married loves: friends among the highest:
prizes: money: international acclaim -

none of them enough. He pushed away
towards the icy drink, the Mississip…
Was he stoned or just gloomily sober
that winter's day in Minnesota,

waving to a passer byeee.

Rathline O' Beirne

We have come to a place of romance,
a beauty spot for dreaming
where men drown.
On the edge of Silver Strand,
my friend and I look down

at the rocks of Rathline O'Beirne.
Out of the sapphire, turquoise,
silver sea, they jut like hulls
of sinking ships. The children
want to frolic, they do not

comprehend the abeyance of forever.
They see only sand the colour
of Spanish gold, the picture book
beauty of a cove, the start
of adventure – never the end.

We stand above a beauty spot,
a place of romance
where men drown.
Rathline O'Beirne was wild
the night Evelyn Marie went down.

St Conal's Island

Bare-footed, the Atlantic
up to my trouser-knees,
I caught a cold on Inniskeel;
cut off, almost, on a heap of rock
consecrated by love's terrible need.

But this was not Lough Derg,
barren of all but guilt
and sin and misery.
Heather and wild daffodils
blossomed. Among bright sods

we trod ancient graves
worn smooth by eleven centuries,
the salt-rain sea, the soles
of pilgrims and tourists,
and doubters just like me.

Seabirds with yellow beaks
spread black wings to fish
and break their bread.
Messengers with a world
to feed, watching from their rock.

All Ireland froze for want of Europe.
But Europe did not freeze.
The sacred flame was cupped
by lonely men like these,
whom you and I tread underfoot.

History, Philosophy, and Italia '90

Warming up for the next encounter
on Italy's fifth green field,
I pitched into Bertrand Russell's
History of Western Philosophy.
News reported the state of play
in Belfast, London, Derry.
...Political disorder
found expression in Machiavelli's
Prince...We'll inflict
worselves on the opposition,
put them under pressure,
said Jack. In Rome,
the Christians would attack.

...In the absence of guiding principles
politics becomes a naked struggle
*for power...*The value of the punt
against lire millionaires:
Cascarino against Baresi.
What happened in Greece
                              happened again
in Renaissance Italy.
Bonner saved but Schillaci scored.

Tense with fury, my friend
deplored the decision and, sensing a plot,
exhorted the IRA
to blow the referee away.
You know me, he said shame-faced.
The rage for justice
explodes traditional constraints,
especially when goalposts are displaced.

...But anarchy and treachery
which resulted in the decay
of morals made Italians impotent,
collectively, and they fell,
like the Greeks, under the domination
of nations less civilised...
The Argentinians.

Collins, Breen and Barry
shot and bombed Britain to treat
for terms. Was it a victory,
stalemate, or tactical
                              retreat?
We lost on penalties.

The Irish dammed O'Connell Street
to welcome home an Englishman,
and celebrate victory
                              in defeat.
Big Jack for President!
God's delight in disillusionment.

Hostages

Curfew sirens wail like women
for their children,
who will not come home.
They have lost the law,
and justice is random.

In the wilderness of the world,
disguised as himself,
he went willingly,
bearing the knowledge
of what must come to pass.
At checkpoints they search uneasily,
on the border they nail the grass.

Is this how you pictured it would be,
among prints of palms
and the light blue Sea of Galilee?
Good little Sunday School soldier
in shirt and tie,
eyes the colour of sky and psalms;
shy in a world of good intentions
and no harm.

Out of the casual crowd
the nervous file appeared:
soldiers surrounded by shoppers,

the last man walking backwards.
They cradled their arms
as though holding babies;
young men mostly,
judging by their faces.
Each soldier wore a tie,
knotted perfectly,
as though each had come
specially dressed for death.

Absolve us from the fate of prey.
On the coffin-black road
from which there is no turning,
we demur in fear and hope.
Some keep a vigil
outside the gates,
for those who follow
and those who wait.

Remove from us the black spot,
upon us bestow the gift of shame.
The shadow of circling wings
lift from our clouded land.

Parable for Would-be Ascetics

On the road to Burtonport,
O'Callaghan on his last legs –
bog-eyed, done in
by the mother of a sleepless night –
discourses upon sin.

Roast lamb, fresh vegetables
or a nice piece of cod
with something dark to cool the heat
would do us both more good.

But, suffering God,
nothing I say
chops the logic
of his pale and freckled monologue.

Man, I privately conclude,
gnaws the bones of all things spiritual.
Tired, he is critical;
but hungry, emphatic.
Ethics on an empty stomach –
food for fanatics.

His condition is serious.
I wish he'd put a sock in it,
be more empirical.
Give the Devil a rest
and me a vacation.

He quotes Temptations,
especially One and Three.
Well, I know some scripture too
although not as much to be
Devil's Advocate,
the role he loves to play.

I am thinking of the fig tree,
that fruitless sinner,
the day troubled Jesus
                              tired and hungry
took the road from Bethany
desperate for dinner.

What good are you to me?
Arid hypocrite,
                 get to Hell!
It did. My friend,
that innocent but lifeless tree
was good
              only for firewood.

Flowers of Ireland

Hedge-fuchsias redder than roses,
brighter than the blood of Enniskillen poppies
and those illuminated bleeding hearts
nailed over photos of the dead Kennedys.

Foxgloves whiter than a taoiseach's lies,
unholy sepulchres. Violet as mascara,
Elizabeth Taylor's eyes,
the steeples of border cathedrals.

Blackthorn jags sharper than triggers,
concealed like forbidden wirelesses
under inhospitable Hawthorn;
the frightened eyes of Irises.

Country Life

I can find no peace in the country
      when unbroken cloud oppresses
the horizon, and sodden trees close
      in their uniform surgical dresses.

The miserable saint of rain has pitched
      her tents of penitence and misery
here. I trespass in this blissful domain,
      counting her tears on the windows.

Blake would have died in the country.
      His Soho garden in Golden Square
was all the nature he deemed necessary.
      Paint and ink his oxygen, not empty air.

Those gushingly wide-open spaces,
      the slightly brown water to drink;
those hectic, flu-reddened faces;
      the headaches that won't let you think.

Powerscourt in Wicklow

Wicklow's flying column hills
are aflame with rape, the colour papal.
Ireland's own Mount Fuji, the Sugarloaf,
reminds me of Rio where urchins,
beyond the Saviour's reach, shame Pelé.

Laurence Olivier confounded the French
at Agincourt with an army of Wicklow

farmers. George Peppard and Anton
Diffring fought dogfights for the sky
Blue Max. Now others prepare.

Powerscourt's walls and wrought-iron gates
preserve the illusion of order.
Inside this enlightened garden state
hardy annuals are self-supporting,
the only borders are herbaceous.

Portuguese standard laurels
resemble the Sun King's orange trees.
Japanese cedars, Californian wellingtonias -
even the conifers are imported.
If only all plantations were as harmonious.

The house, Palladian, was designed by Castle.
His German passion for obelisks and eagles
pre-dates Speer by sixty years.
The bronzed pegasi were cast in Germany
before the Franco-Prussian War.

Into the belly of the innocent air
a minor sea god shoots just spray.
Fire gutted the house on Guy Fawkes Day.
Inside immaculate ruins, unruly nature
violates elegant rooms where the monied

and the great struck matches, and arranged
affairs of state. Foliage rustles silkily
on inlaid floors. In place of the Lancers,
the Foxtrot, the clatter of beaks
and talons, the furtive scraping of claws.

Dark Thoughts

Sackcloth cannot be as black
as the bloody heart
of rural Ireland.
After lights out
it's as pitch as England
the year Shakespeare
wrote King Lear.

Fear of things unseen
intensifies the night.
In the garden with a Hamlet
I duck as headlights
distantly rake
the dark's angles,
as though searching for
Dorniers and Heinkels.

Clever De Valera
kept the State free
of England's war.
Our misfortune:
Ireland's opportunity.
They buried their guns
in shallow graves,
the easier to retrieve
to make more widows grieve.

Now index fingers twitch
for Deutschmarks and modernity.
Ah, but who could unite
Ireland like Germany?
The Irish love disorder,
besides, there is
money in the border.

Oscar

No longer the poseur
in the green carnation:
the cabaret is over.
Clapped out on English
railway stations,
remembering the stages
by which he rose and fell.
Another Irish writer,
unwise but witty,
dying in a country
less foreign than his own.

8. From **LEARNING THE CRAFT**

History

Time stands still for the clock-making king
between the legs of Madame Guillotine.

A whiff of grapeshot blasts the Rights of Man,
France opens her legs to a Corsican.

Under Little Caesar's eagles Europa roars,
Picasso paints *The Disasters of War.*

Victor Hugo stares into the maddened Atlantic.
Russia industrialises – the Tsar's Titanic

steams impressively towards Tsushima Straits.
Holed up in Zurich, Ulyanov waits

for an armoured train. Jewish Gustav Mahler
makes his peace with Martin Luther.

The Maxim replaces the Guillotine,
Nijinsky dances Europe's *Rite of Spring.*

New nations form, old borders disappear,
Kafka ghosts through Prague holding Van Gogh's ear.

Proust wears yellow gloves in bed while he
remembers how things used to be.

Freud discovers America while a blue guitar
strums the sound of music Da-Da Da-Da.

On Rhode Island, Long Island, the craze is cash
the latest dance is the Wall Street Crash.

Seurat's placid bathers are certified insane.
Condors shadow encircled cities in Spain.

Not for the first time Poland is partitioned,
Bismarck's Ironclads are reconditioned.

King Ubu parades in a bullet-proof car,
Goya paints over *Guernica*.

Münch screams unheard in a fog-filled fjord.
Tolstoy dies in the station at Buchenwald.

Baudelaire's digging skeletons complete
Neville Chamberlain's winding sheet.

The past is embalmed or else abolished,
countries and churches are demolished,

faces are erased from photographs,
asylums are places where doctors laugh.

Through smoking badlands Marshall rides,
Dakotas replenish Germany's starving tribes.

Between Dallas and Hanoi that will change,
and outlaws pacify the range.

Caesar walls off East Berlin
to keep the happy Communists in.

Sparta against Athens protects its flanks,
Budapest then Prague are filled with tanks.

Kennedy's Lincoln becomes his hearse,
Géricault's horse follows, boots reversed.

Sayonara to time say the rays of the sun:
the Enola Gay and Little Boy come.

Amsterdam

A Fokker Friendship brings me down
to a land of fluorescent strips.
It's an exhibition of parallel lines –
Van Gogh eclipsed by Mondrian.

At Schiphol propellers windmill to a stop,
asterisks become CND signs.
Blue men armed with automatics
do not invite tourists to ask the time.

Amsterdam is a NOW city
the brochure assures me. Pity.
Cross your bridges or burn them,
Amsterdam has a thousand to choose from.

Canals moat fortress apartment blocks.
Spires tower medievally
between neon ads for cars and clocks.
City of Rembrandt and Johann Cruyff,

overhead wires and wavering lines –
a Bridget Riley made of steel.
Bicycles, dykes, houseboats and junkies:
everything floats or turns on wheels.

At Leidesplein youths on saxophone and drums
improvise delirium in the open air.
Stately facades are canvasses for graffiti.
Amsterdam is more than a city,

it's a state of mind.
In a bar off Rembrandtstraat
Salome smiles and asks lonely men
if they find the city *naughty.*

Behind the eyes of glamorous tarts
and the strip-lighting of bars
silence seeks asylum from the past.
Tram tracks are arterial scars.

Intent on being NOW every minute,
Amsterdam tries to connect.
Plenty of LIVE FUCKING, says the sign
for those who want to forget.

Amsterdam, I cannot tell if you are ahead
or behind. Tomorrow it is summertime.
Tonight, six floors above it,
I look down in the rain.

In the dark of the canal
a mallard looks up at what I see
and, through midnight's honking traffic,
cackles somewhat derisively.

Asylum

Van Gogh!
The English woman
glanced up from her history.
Wasn't he the one
who went completely mad?
Such is the nature
of museums,
asylums.

The pastor thought he might be,
as did the Ministers
who dismissed his ministry
in the coalfields of the Borinage.
Only the miners who worked the galleries,
potato-eaters, did not deny him.
Unlike the dealers in London and Paris,
women, and most of his teachers.

From the cold fields of the North
he fled South to the Yellow House
on the Place Lamartine.
A thin fox of a man
whose green eyes
were sometimes blue,
whose convict stubble
scorched to a crop
brighter than wheatfields.

Café at Night

To you, O Lord, I come
burning to serve.
I offer this gold, this blue:
my brushes are candles
alight with paint.

Sorrow

This is my body:
you can have it
for a bottle of wine
or the price of a meal.
Stroke it, stoke it,
it will respond.
Bend it, break it,
it will come to heel.
You want a piece
of the action?
Have a piece of me
and, since love
cannot be requited,
keep it.

The Sower

I labour like the peasant,
sowing the earth
to give succour to the ones
who do not reap love
beneath God's sun.

Potato Eaters

No light of Vermeer
or any of those Dutch Masters
orders this interior.
They crouch as though underground,
sharing a subterranean stable.

They know of cunning and hardship,
they know how to survive,
breaking the heartless earth
and the fruits of it:
a crock of lumpy potatoes
between a family of five.

A woman whose face
has been mined of nobility
which suffering's supposed to bestow,
eyes me craftily
as she pours thick black coffee.

Her husband proffers a potato.
It gleams like an unearthed rock
under the lamp's sickly halo.

Van Gogh's Museum

At the Yellow House in Arles
they queued to mock the freak,
who carved off half an ear
as a farmer would withered wheat.

He said his soul was a house
where fire blazed at the hearth,
but no one knocked at the door
to warm their hands at its heart.

In the madhouse at St Rémy
he painted fields through bars,
filling them with houses and people
and overhead whirling stars.

The world was a vacant house
he tried to warm with his heat.
On an empty day he shot himself
in a field of wounded wheat.

The Last Train is Always Leaving

Rain falls on Amsterdam
with military precision.
Vast squares are cleared
as though by air attack.
I duck the tracers
between dismal ranks of trees
marshalled on Museumplein
like anxious refugees.

It could be a morning in Poland,
a station waiting for trains.

Tomorrow, on churches
banks and public buildings,
in every cellar and bar,
hands will be pushed forward
to recapture an hour.
Now turn all clocks back,
for I have a train to catch.

I join the queue to get in
Prisengracht 263.
A narrow scaffold of stairs
pushes me vertically
towards a trapdoor
and little rooms
hidden faithfully by books.
Noisily we inspect the quarters
which hid eight for three years.
Through windows with green frames
the street's freedom shines,
absolved by rain.
Bullet holes appear in the black canal,
umbrellas parachute open,
lovers clutch each other
and run for cover.
There is a trapdoor in the sky
where God hides.
She should have been sixteen,
she would have scattered flowers
from Amsterdam to Normandy.
Rejoicing to be alive
she would have teased
despairing boyfriends.

There is a photograph of a neat list.
Across it in line abreast
names ruled out neatly.
This is the last train's manifest.

In the red light district
it is Friday night.

Red bulbs glow
brighter than tulips.
Nude women stare from boxrooms
no bigger than the ones
from which I have come.
Some smile at the window-shoppers,
others disdain the parade.
Now Germans return
in Mercedes and Daimlers.
This time it is no sin
if this woman looks Jewish
or that one has a dark skin.

After polishing off a large meal
a man asked a waiter
where he could see
A lady in a box.
I should have told him
Prisengracht 263.

Tonight a five star box
takes me from the rain;
but tonight I am still leaving
on Anne Frank's last train.

Breakfast in Utrecht

Hunched over beers
in the café called Extase,
each of us submerged
as rain darkens
the streets of memory.
Grey as an aircraft carrier,
the day is sailing away.
Like a soldier
missing his country,
or a lover
missing another,
part of me longs to go
and part of me wants to stay
in Extase forever,
with beer for company
and rain, sailing
just sailing away.

The Dark Satellite

In war's great hungry time, when farmlands
fed by incessant shot and shell no longer sang,
he begged his way across country, the lanes
well-rutted by Prussian Uhlans and artillery.

Under harsh Northern skies he scraped his soles,
wading red seas of wheat, the roads
a tourniquet of wounded men and horses.
Citadels were aflame, Heaven's bell rang

vain tocsins among siege-towers of cloud.
Once upon a time a boy might bivouac
below camp fires of the Bear and eat his share,
content to let the Plough direct his wandering.

Then, how easy it was to believe and dream
of mighty orchestral mountains Hannibal had crossed;
a secret lake, a lagoon of masts; a forest of eyes
and, as always, a child happy to be lost.

Through fields of bayonets and marshalling yards
to sullen provincial towns, brooding in musty libraries,
following camel routes to ancient desert cities
ungoverned by kings or tutting librarians.

Now the forest is drowned by fogs.
Rhabdomancers entice the gullible to black streams
of amnesia, lethal ponds frequented by child-murderers;
the holy elixir spiked by charlatans,

poisoning the streams he drank from.
To such places nothing natural longs to slake its thirst.
The sun itself is cursed and carbonises the world,
daisies manufacture malignancies.

Far from the boredom and uncertainty of war,
sick, self-hating, drunk with sadness and maladies,
he follows the piccolo between foul alleys.
From mustard and rape rank odours of homicide

roll through splintered valleys.
Inspiration's mortal crystals are pestled,
syphoned through a nest of tubes to retorts
where everything pure is boiled away.

Innocence is baked into cakes and slipped
under children's tongues by spiteful nurses;
the whole ensemble accompanied by a military band.
From these nightmares laureates fashion heroic verses

as the stars are dismantled and borders locked.
Europe's marble mantelpiece, thick with dust
and fingerprints, is robbed of magnificent candlesticks;
embossed invitations burn in the grate.

The sewer stench of the Mediterranean inflames
a diseased imagination with toxic potions.
Dreaming of undeciphered Rosetta Stones
he crosses the Red Sea, in Aden finds his wilderness,

in the scarred hands of Ethiopia he drives his nail.
Like a star in a well out of sight of Heaven;
thwarted, plagued, and lonely; cut off in Marseilles
where the Sisters of Mercy attend his terrible wound.

Cockroaches

Cockroaches are immune to radiation.

Nothing moves, they say, in Pripyat;
no one makes love or money.
> Cardiograph machines declare
> no human heart beats there.

The entire town is a hope-free zone,
no need to plan for the future.
> Imperatives like *should* and *must*
> are sticks and stones in dust.

Time stands still in Pripyat's
radioactive habitat.
> In time, a thousand years or so,
> the town might make a come-back.

Pompeii staged a recovery
from the dead; Nagasaki thrives.
    Not much chance for Krakatoa
    though; au revoir to Muraroa.

What is history without folk?
A ghost town where shirts and frocks
    flap uncollected in the wind,
    and none can be taken in.

One boon of radiation –
no queues for accommodation.
    No more critics, no more dissent;
    mail's uncensored though unsent.

Men other than pharoahs also knew
a scarab's talismanic value.
    Long before nuclear fusion,
    Kafka reached the same conclusion.

Metamorphosis, Franz implied,
was Mankind's best way to survive
    alpha, beta, gamma rays.
    Crawling, as we know, sometimes pays.

Should Repin or Norman Rockwell
return to paint this side of Hell,
    realism is out. Pripyat
    provides, like a vast reproach,

the symbol for our age: the roach.
Remember this, lest we forget,
    in spite of Pripyat and Chernobyl
    la cucaracha, ignoble

ghost in the modern machine
(victimised and called unclean),
    smaller than both rat and gannet,
    survives the monsters of this planet.

Learning the Craft

Easier than you or I can see
a Page Three model
conceal herself in nudity,
Michelangelo saw the Piéta
buried in a block of stone.

In the hot quarries of Carrara,
learning the craft alone,
he laboured to earn the grace
to liberate life and carve
a human smile on a marble face.

Letter to W.H. Auden

Fifty years ago you quaked in that dive
on New York's 52nd Street, drink
in hand; uncertain, afraid, but alive.
Did you feel a refugee or a fink
as Hitler kicked Europe over the brink?
And that rough beast which Yeats foresaw
slouching towards Bethlehem fed in Warsaw.

I must confess to doubts about your role,
you who denounced the *international wrong,*
the hero in the bar enjoying parole
from Guderian's tanks and Göring's bombs
in America. You did not belong.
On Fire Island with the fruits of fame,
how easy to show an *affirming flame*

while Hitler blitzed your home. Clever friends
explained your exile. I can understand
up to a point; but I cannot pretend
to admire what seems to me underhand,
and you a poet. But I remain a fan,
especially of your pre-war verse
which makes the familiar new, not perverse.

Your penchant for flippancy, at times a strain,
is never less than human and often true.
Loquacious, audacious, appalled by pain,
you auditioned words and rejected few.
Though poetry should have a point of view
it should not wave flags for every public cause.
Annihilating all that's made to a clause –

whether Four or Twenty-eight. Poetry
should not be held hostage to a thought.
If all art is propaganda, as Trotsky said,
fortunately yours falls some way short
of old hat. Revolutionary catharsis,
let's be blunt, is fillip for guys who
don't change nappies or never have to.

Stalin, Hitler, Pol Pot, Mao Tse-Tung:
every monster starts off a hero,
then tries to stop the clock; has writers hanged
and critics shot. Each has his own *Year Zero.*
I don't suppose that civilised Plato
would have found a place for Mandelstam
in his Republic. Poetry alarms

warped and wounded thought that struts in mufti.
Though verses did nothing to save Anne Frank
they are dangerous – ask Salman Rushdie.
Poetry did not prevent Belsen for cranks
love murder more; but words turned back tanks
in Tiananmen. Sin and human error
crush poets as much as boredom or terror,

but poetry flows on through the death camps,
those *ranches of despair and isolation.*
It is the flame on candles and in lamps
that flickers and flares amid desolation,
even in New York. No explanation
that I can offer will suffice:
the loveless long to put the world to rights.

Europe is volatile and uncertain
as it was fifty years ago; but Yalta
no longer defines the Iron Curtain.
The Warsaw Pact is dead. Psalter
and Bible like grass grow stronger.
Uprooted from plinth and pedestal,
it is the men of iron and steel who fall

from the Baltic to the Danube. Faith
rolls back the stone; the past is exhumed
and truth uncovered like mass graves.
From Moscow to East Berlin secret rooms
are broken open like Egyptian tombs,
buried but not forgotten. Coast to coast,
in from the cold comes the Holy Ghost.

Ideas don't need passports, they travel light.
With fear and hope men and women call;
history moves on; the moving finger writes
a fiery warning on the Berlin Wall.
Behind the thunder of the waterfall,
the cave of illusion and reality
gives up its inmates to posterity.

September 1989

Autumn Statement

I: Paddington

Isambard Kingdom Brunel gazes stony-faced
from his black throne, as Friday commuters
hurry from Elizabeth Bishop's hits
orbiting the Circle Line. The blue train to Oxford
has been stationary since four. It's after six,
we go for a bitter. A coin activates the jukebox:
Should I Stay or Should I Go?
Negotiating barrows of fruit and flowers
I ask a patrolling policeman.
He is curious but does not know.

II: Remembering Auden at Oxford

My eyes rake quads of medieval halls.
Above Christ Church's leprous walls
Peter points out the arthritic slates
of Auden's cottage, his home in Sixty-five.
Mr W.H. Grease-proof paper creases
in his face. Behind shipping magnate's
shades, donned for the camera, the eyes
of an exile. Auden felt out of place,
alone at his afternoon table at St Aldate's.
Revered but not respected, like tradition,
the royal family or a bloody college.
There are good reasons for hating people,
especially those in pursuit of knowledge.

III: Looking for Louis MacNeice

Blackwell's depresses me
more than Oxford's college quads.
Its students and tutors,
better read than Shakespeare,
should be forced to strip
car engines at Cowley.
Men who hope to be mistaken for professors
linger over Philip Larkin's
bald ungenerous letters.
Thin apostle of arsenic and old lace,
who makes charity coagulate.
They mull in sherried vein
as I ransack the shelves in vain
for red-blooded Louis MacNeice.

IV: The Ghost of Juliette Greco

Abstracted
in something black
and off-the-shoulder,
the ghost of Juliette Greco
stands hand on heart in Browns.
Alone and pale and scary,
a silhouette against the light,
she wears a crimson velvet hat,

the brim pinned back.
A cross between a Bowery bum
and a Millet's Pre-Raphaelite
in lycra, waiting for someone
to murder her or buy her lunch.

V: At Shelley's Monument

Mick Jagger unconsciously caught
the spirit of your naughtiness,
reciting Adonais in a white dress.
Truly, you came of age in 1969
among the painted paper faces.
University College also unconsciously
caught the spirit of your poetry
in its sickly marmoreal monument.

VI: Don

Profitably flows the modern Don
writing, talking, on and on.
Lucky the branch of knowledge
that he descends upon.
Feathering his nest in a college,
as sure of himself as a swan.
Where would Oxford be without him?
The country would surely go wrong,
the Civil Service would founder,
the Government wouldn't last long,
who would ruin the Bank of England,
or disorganise poor Hong Kong.
Education would go for a burton,
erudition would be sold for a gong.
All Souls may be empty of students
and Somerville vacant of Johns,
but the world is his oyster,
his quad and his cloister,
just as long as he answers to Don.

VII: The Last Afternoon

England darkens. On the last afternoon,
from the top of the Tower
of the Four Winds,
where the Thames knots Oxford's throat
and unfarmed country begins,
I see the end of cultivated minds.

The bicycling figure of spinsterish Starkie,
Rimbaud's midwife on heat with love
that cannot be requited:
sad Isaiah, with his memories
of Pasternak and tragic Akhmatova,
walled up in these palaces of preferment.

Would I have found a friend for life,
like minds worth sharing?
Now, like a forlorn Inspector Morse
I sit alone, winter gaslight
reflecting faces in a glass of red,
with only dead friends for company.

In the Country of René Magritte

I: Above Places of Exile and Defeat

On the starboard wing Dunkirk
and to port Ostend.
Aviation fuel from fallen fighters and bombers
colours the English Channel.

The higher you are
the slower things seem;
everything is relative
when you travel

above places of exile and defeat.
William the Conqueror
passes Ike's invasion fleet,
as Blériot just misses a Spitfire.

II: Spring's Offensive

Luxembourg retreats
as we advance on Brussels
through the ghost front of three generations:
the Ardennes, lair of the boar
and the Royal King Tiger.

Spring's offensive is late;
Montgomery to Anderlecht
parks are muddy after-thoughts,
untended beds of green-grocery.
They dig vegetables not flower gardens,
and know the value of deep trenches,
machinery. Faces like potatoes,
but minds of rubber and ivory.
They cut diamonds on their only coast
and brew four hundred kinds of beer.
They like their songs like their chocolate:
bitter and dark but sweet.

Caxton's first book was printed here,
Dutch Erasmus had a garden where
Thomas More's Utopia - paradise
for fools - preceded Vanity Fair.

III: Courts of Justice

Inspired by Greece
but admired by Hitler,
the pompous contours
of the Courts of Justice
remind me of the Graf Spee,
Scharnhorst, the Admiral Scheer.
Like Neo-Classical artillery,
its double columns flatten
all argument and doubt.
Linz would have looked like this:
the world would have looked like Linz.

IV: The Magicians of Brussels

Geneva of Northern Europe:
lakeless, horizontal,
without Calvinists or movie stars.
City of gables, attics
and legerdemain.
A brass plate on a wizened
green door announces
the domain of Doctor Merlin.
Quicker than I can spell
Thierry Boutsen or Jacky Ickx,
an illusionist on Grand Place
transforms twelve flags
into a gas-ring of golden stars.
The Commission's
seventeen magicians
transmute the base carrot
into Portuguese fruit.
By sleight of hand
all borders vanish,
except those in the mind.
In the country of René Magritte
reality is negotiable.

V: In the Military Museum

The after-lunch slowness
of European afternoons.
Great planes and chestnuts
suffocate like Ney's dragoons
under their weight of plumage,
bottle-green, indigo and blue.
We go to inspect the military museum
to kill an hour or two.

Among mangling trench mortars,
the iron-mongery of black howitzers
field guns and siege cannon,
cast at Liège and fired at Ypres,
I try to feel duly solemn,
try to interest myself in precision
engineering, the ingenuity
which cancelled battalions, divisions.

But the omnipresence of machinery
makes my mind wander from the mess
bequeathed by tanks and artillery,
to trees in summer battledress
and to gold-coloured tricolours.
Blue as the eyes of provincial conscripts,
whiter than the eyes of the enemy,
red as the blood which slipped

under the feet of falling men
in fields of rye and bitter barley
at Waterloo, on the road to Brussels.
Tom, Tom. Here come the Calvary!
A drummer boy's unintentional irony
comes back to me in the sun,
as we tread aimlessly among debris
of Scorpion, Panther, and Centurion.

VI: *The Metropole's Dancing Waiters*

More sure of themselves than Jesuits
and gigolos, the Metropole's dancing waiters
fandango between marble mirrors,
pillars, and quilted upholstery.
In a whirl of waistcoats and aprons
they balance glass models of Manhattan
on circular trays with four fingers.
Invariably locating the right place,
if they do get an order wrong
you apologise for your mistake.

VII: *A Louer*

One of René Magritte's
bowler-hatted insurance men
will drop the universe,
no bigger than a ball,
into his briefcase.
On the windowsill of the dark
and starless vacancy
he'll place a card:
a louer. And nobody
will notice.

VIII: Taxi Driver

My Luxembourg cabbie is bilingual
and probably ambidextrous.
He drives a black Sierra,
tunes the radio and smokes a Camel.
I'm an Englishman in New York.
Hannibal Lecter wins the Oscar

bravo.

IX: Charlie's Café

Through the big picture window
of Charlie's Café
Brussels is a charcoal sketch
on sugarbag-blue paper.

I order another Becks
to get a close-up
of the intense waitress
who looks like Edith Piaf.

She rarely smiles
and never stops moving.
If this place is a desert to her
it is my oasis.

I could sit here forever,
watching the dessert cool
in its tub of ice,
like John Mills in Alex.

Full-bodied Stella
has made me starry-eyed.
She brings me coffee from Africa,
as hot and horny as the Cape.

X: Shoes

Female foreign journalists
in chic outfits and expensive shoes
click over impeccable parquet
in the European Parliament.
I'd fall in love but lack the leather.

XI: Tristesse

On the Place St Catherine
there is a white tower
without a bell.

Life is fruitless and rueful
and slightly untruthful.
I can go no further
on the Rue de l'Amigo.

XII: Premonition

I sweat in my Brussels' hotel bed,
throat parched and wide awake.
Monet's Impression of Sunrise
a bullet wound above my head.
Muzzle-flashes startle dogs
maddened by a fusillade of thunder.
From Montgomery to Sarajevo
the sky splits asunder
as it did on the eve of Waterloo.
Europe's grand illusion quakes.
Lightning's premonition hangs over all
the salt water smell of fate.

9. REMEMBRANCE SUNDAY

I. Age Shall Not Weary Them, Nor the Years Condemn.

Narrator:-

I don't know where they got the steel
that, fashioned into bolts, locked
bullets into place for firing.
I don't know where they got the cloth
woven by women which others cut
and dyed and sewed men into uniforms.
I don't know who made the rules,
for rules are not made like men
or steel or bullets or cloth.
I don't know why the war was fought:
who won, who lost; nor what was gained
which lasted. We must not count the cost.
Nor do I know where love comes from,
which made the men whom others
roped to posts at dawn and shot.
I don't know why tears fill my eyes
when, on Remembrance Sunday, I hear
the Last Post at the Cenotaph.
Is it because the collective ache
of remembering, the communion of loss,
binds me to the nation as to a stake?
Each in his solitude bears a cross
and joins the pale battalions
marching, a hundred paces to the minute.
A military band plays Nimrod
as the dismembered cavalcade of dead
whom England bore, shaped, made aware,
pass by like wrongs hushed up.
Big Ben strikes eleven times.
They watch us stand with lowered heads
wondering: Is it shame or respect
that wets our eyes as we remember?

Court Martial. The Prosecutor says (it is an actual quote):-

From the evidence produced, the accused is evidently a worthless soldier with no heart for fighting. I consider that the tendency to plead that the effects of a shell bursting near an individual is an excuse for the worst crime a soldier can commit and requires severe examples to be carried out. *Voice of firing squad officer. A volley of shots echoes and merges into the sound of a salute by field artillery on Remembrance Sunday. In turn, this sound merges into the solemn beat of a muffled drum.*

The Narrator:- During the Great War, 307 soldiers from Britain and its Empire were shot at dawn for offences against the Military Act. These crimes included throwing away a weapon (*the voice of the Prosecutor screams* "Funk!"), sleeping on duty (*the Prosecutor screams* "Skrimshanker!"), leaving the post ("Lead-swinger!"), cowardice ("Malingerer!"), and desertion ("Shirker!"). Only two of the 307 were officers. Many of the others were volunteers. Some of these had been rejected on medical grounds, only to be conscripted after the slaughter of the first two years on the Western Front. Others joined up from a sense of duty. One such was Harry MacDonald, a 32-year-old family man from Keighley, near Bradford. In 1914 he joined the 12th Battalion of the West Yorkshire Regiment, number 43665, in spite of his wife's protestations.

II. But Who Can Judge Him – You or I?

Lily MacDonald:–

Where is his place in this parade?
He didn't hide inside his conscience,
behind the baby's cot or my skirts.
He left his work at the foundry
and took the oath at the Hall.

You're too old for soldiering, I told him.
He was thirty, we'd wed the year before.
I can't turn my back on my country,
he said. Lily, this is war!
You've four mouths to feed, I said.
But I was eight years younger,
and he had fought the Boers.

I had twenty-seven shillings a week –
the Army called it Separation Pay.

They sent him to Gallipoli,
I had to laugh; he rarely
went as far as Leeds.

They sent him home with lice, frostbite.
I thought it was hot in Turkey.
Under my feet for a month or two,
I didn't think he was right.
He wasn't happy. I was poorly,
expecting. He thought it wasn't his.
You need me by you! he kept saying,
and begged for a bit more leave.
Chaps in red caps came to fetch him.
They sent him to the Somme.

That July, the Telegraph was black with photographs:
West Riding's missing and wounded, the dead.
Good-looking lads mostly;
the men had moustaches like Harry.
Some were his pals, but he was not among them.
I knew something was wrong
because it wasn't in the paper.

A chaplain called Jackman wrote.
Harry, he said, had passed away.
He sent me his paybook and badges,
but they stopped his pension and his pay.

I had to go to the workhouse.
I got thirteen-and-six a week
for clothing, food and rent.

The Narrator:–

Harry MacDonald was an experienced soldier, well aware of the
rigours of Army discipline. And yet he deserted twice. The first time
he failed to report back from leave and was arrested by the Military
Police. He was given Field Punishment Number One: handcuffed to
the wheels of a gun-carriage for two hours a day in full view of his
comrades. He was sent to the Front in July 1916 and was buried alive
by a German shell. Treatment at base hospital was cursory; before
long he was despatched to the forward trenches again. Knowing that
desertion would mean certain death, nevertheless he ran for a second

time, towards England and his pregnant wife. He was arrested on September 12, near Boulogne, a coastal sector heavily-patrolled by Red Caps, court-martialled and sentenced to death. Seemingly an open and shut case. But the court recommended clemency, a recommendation ignored by the military authorities. The Army doctor dismissed Harry MacDonald's case as "an attack of cowardly imagination." His company commander said Private MacDonald was "worthless. Of no fighting value." He was shot at dawn on Saturday, November 4 – Our Heroes' Bairns Flag Day back in Bradford.

Lily MacDonald:–

I remarried and got away.
Questions were asked in Parliament.

The Narrator:–

In May 1915 Robert Graves, an officer in the Royal Welch Fusiliers, had his first direct experience of what he later called "official lying". He had arrived back at rest camp in Le Havre and was reading the back-file of Army orders.

Robert Graves:–

They contained something like twenty reports of men shot at dawn for cowardice or desertion; yet a few days later the minister responsible in the House of Commons, answering a question from a pacifist, denied that sentence of death for a military offence had been carried out in France on any member of His Majesty's Forces.

The Narrator:–

Harry MacDonald is buried at Louvencourt Military Cemetery, France. Plot 1, row D, grave 17.

III. The Air is Loud with Death.

Heavy rifle and machine-gun fire, shells exploding. The Narrator speaks the following six lines matter-of-factly, as though setting an exam question on the causes of the First World War.

What remains of a man
after jagged fragments
of exploding shell
have punctured his body
and shattered the casing
that contains his mind?

The Narrator continues:–

Private Charles McColl, second of the Cenotaph's ghostly cavalcade,
speaks his mind.

McColl:–

I went out of mine
when the Somme entered it
that morning over the top.
Sixty thousand of us copped it.
I was shipped home to Yorkshire
with more wounds than Jesus.

They knew bloody well
something else was wrong,
but sent me back to the Front
in 1917. I couldn't control
the battle in my head.
I got out of it.

Four days on the run.
They said our generals
were thirty miles behind us.
I didn't see one.

The Narrator:–

Private Charles McColl, 1-4 East Yorkshire Regiment, service
number 11/81, was captured and, without either medical
examination or legal counsel, court-martialled and sentenced.

McColl:–

Even Christ had an advocate.
I can find nothing wrong with him, said Pilate.

That's what they made out about me.
I tried to explain, but the big guns
wouldn't listen. Three days after Christmas
they had me shot. I was twenty-six.

Captain C. S. Slack MC, from McColl's regiment:–

There was one poor little man who came to see me. He was a half-
wit. It was getting on in the war and we were getting very poor
material out, and he was posted to my Company and he ran away, and
he was caught and ran away again, deserted, and he was court-
martialled to be shot. I had to pick, with my Sergeant Major, ten men
to shoot him, which we did. I wrote to his mother, "Killed in action",
and I think that's what they were told in every case. One didn't give
them details as to how people were killed. I wasn't present at the
execution. I didn't want to be.

The Narrator:–

Charles McColl is buried at Ypres Reservoir Cemetery, Belgium. Plot
4, row A, grave 6.

IV. Remember Happy England.

The Narrator:–

Remember sickly Louis Harris
whose family lived in Leeds?
He tried to enlist in 1915,
twenty-one and dead keen
to be a Kitchener Blue.
They failed him at the medical:
unfit to die for his country.

Six out of nine Englishmen
were given the bullet,
saved from death temporarily
by TB, rickets, malnutrition.
But Ypres, Arras and Loos,
then Haig's Big Push in 1916
crippled or killed the volunteers.
Low on human ammunition,
they had to conscript.

The standard was lowered;
they privateered Louis Harris,
and though unfit he served two years.

Louis Harris, proudly:–

Service number 43055, 10th West Yorkshire Regiment.

The Narrator:–

The month the fighting was stopped,
the week before Armistice,
they charged him with desertion.

Louis Harris:–

In the month of the dead

The Narrator:–

A grateful nation shot him.
He was twenty-three.

Louis Harris is buried at the British Cemetery, Ghissignies, France.
Row B, grave 34. He was the last British soldier to be executed in the
Great War.

V. Expression of War Experience.

The Narrator:–

Louis Harris was a year younger than 24-year-old shell shock victim
Second Lieutenant Wilfred Owen, 2nd Battalion, Manchester
Regiment; but Owen was treated rather differently. The view passed
down to us is that little was known about shell shock at that time. This
is the usual explanation for the fate of squaddies like Harry
MacDonald, Charles McColl and Louis Harris. Yet by 1916 medical
specialists had their own word for the condition: Neurasthenia.
Netley Hospital in Hampshire, to which Owen was sent on his return
from France, had specially adapted doors and windows to absorb
noise. Shell shock victims could not abide noise. Shell shock or
neurasthenia is more than a nervous disorder with psychological
consequences; prolonged exposure to bombardment may also burst

eardrums, causing temporary or permanent loss of hearing. Balance is also impaired. In 1992 Dr Charles Vise, ear-nose-and-throat specialist at Bradford Royal Infirmary, was still being consulted by ex-servicemen who had survived the German bombing of Dunkirk more than fifty years earlier. Shell shock was not unknown during the Great War. On November 2nd, 1916, two days before Harry MacDonald's execution, the Bradford Daily Telegraph advertised Dr Williams' "Pink pills for pale people" under the headline: BEWARE OF NEURASTHENIA. What was evident was the different kind of treatment accorded by the Army to neurasthenic officers and ordinary rankers prone to attacks of "cowardly imagination". Just outside Edinburgh a crumbling Victorian health and recreation hydro was turned over to the military from 1916 to 1919 for the treatment of shell shocked officers like Wilfred Owen. Craiglockhart War Hospital for Neurasthenic Officers, now Napier University, was over-crowded and rat-infested; but Owen was fortunate to be there from late June to the end of October 1917. During those four months he met dissident soldier-poet Second Lieutenant Siegfried Sassoon. Sassoon had openly criticised the Allies' conduct of the war in a letter to The Times; rather than risk a scandal by charging Sassoon with treachery his superiors despatched him to Craiglockhart. Under Sassoon's critical eye, Owen was transformed from a derivative writer of poetic sonnets to a war poet. His physical distance from the war and the sixteen months of his recuperation (Owen's biographers offer no explanation for this extenuated leave) only intensified his preoccupation with the realities of battle and its human consequences. At Craiglockhart, Owen began to use words and phrases such as "slob their relish", "stuttering", "demented", "wailing", "blood-shod", "vile, incurable sores", "gargling from froth-corrupted lungs", "waterfalls of slime", "thumping", "deluging", and "shrieking".

The ghost of Wilfred Owen stammers the following poem which opens at Napier University. The sounds of university life form a background to Owen's monologue. He traverses the grounds and buildings remembering Craiglockhart and his time in the trenches.

Siegfried called it Dottyville;
but this dull billet
was my university.
I do not recognise the faces
I see now: young men,
unravaged or numbed

by multitudinous murders.
I see what I might have become.

The lad from Shropshire:
the parson's agnostic assistant:
the Flying Corps flop:
the infantryman
blown into the air
by a random whizz-bang.
Landing here
           I found my feet.

Unshod by Army issue,
they were warm and always dry.
I missed the spring offensive,
the tongueless mouths of mud
that swallowed men wholesale
at Ypres and Passchendaele.
Without even a Blighty
or bar of gold
           to justify my convalescence.
I was lucky, don't ask me why.

Unlike the sodden squaddies
cornered by hellfire or sucked under
by donkeyloads of kit.
A once-over by an orderly,
shot of Navy Rum, cotton wool
to plug their damaged ears,
then up the line again
to face the music;
muddy duckboards cracking underfoot.
Violet-scented air
turning brass buttons green
burned their faces.
Yellow flares
bent them stumbling
into foul and stinking places,
while I settled myself in a chair,
waiting for a space
nearer the fire.

I left my platoon
in a dark and dangerous wood.
I smell their blood in Champagne,
the wheatlands of Lorraine.
I dreamed of them often,
saw their faces grinning
back at me in the pierglass.
Station whistles at Waverley
brought them over the top of mailbags.
People must have thought me mad,
in my blue arm-band and white tab.
At cock-crow I heard reveille.
I knew death was waiting,
the hooded nurse behind the screen,
I was not deceived.
On parole from the wood, my blood waiting to escape
through some dark and secret hole.
Paroled but not reprieved.

What's my reputation now,
three-quarters of a century
after my little leaf
joined the khaki compost heap?
Do they think me a realist,
mistaking me for Siegfried?
Do they think of us together,
confusing my lines with his?

Even at his angriest Siegfried
was at home in the world,
never less than himself.
Whereas I, the stammering man
shy with secrets, tried to lose myself
in aesthetics - until I saw the amputees,
the art of prosthetics.

I see them once again,
shells of men whose minds
the dead had ravished,
withdrawn behind silent doors.
Shadows in twilight
by the bowling green.
Negatives exposed to light,

deafened and made dumb
by the business of bullets.
I see what I might have become.

I had sixteen months of lies
before love drove me back to hell,
to seek forgiveness in their tortured eyes.

VI. In a Place Apart When the Dawn was Grey.

Charles McColl and Louis Harris speak these verses in turn.

Ten rifles point like Kitchener,
but the condemned doesn't see
the finger or the face
reject him like a cartridge case.

> A Lee-Enfield weighs nine pounds:
> the bullets travel thirty miles a minute:
> a lifetime takes a single round.

For the encouragement of others
his hands are tied, his eyes are bound.
Voiceless and blind: obedience
drilled into him like a bullet.
The last word he hears…

> In some secluded corner
> of a foreign field
> they lay their guilt to rest.

Killed in Action, say the telegrams home:
Shot at Dawn, the tablets of stone:
Jerked to Jesus while the day was dark.
The King's Shilling in his pocket,
British bullets in his heart.

VII. Who Goes to Join the Men of Agincourt?

The Narrator:–

Autumn 1916. With the human cost of the war evident in the growing
number of coffins in regional newspapers, The Morning Post tried to
keep the patriotic home fires burning by publishing A Message to the

Trenches by "A Little Mother". In spite of its peculiar imagery this anonymous epistle was later printed as a pamphlet in an edition of 75,000.

For ironic effect, this excerpt from A Message to the Trenches should be read by Lily MacDonald.

There is only one temperature for the women of the British race, and that is white heat. We women pass on the human ammunition of 'only sons' to fill up the gaps, so that when the 'common soldier' looks back before going 'over the top' he may see the women of the British race at his heels...We would have much preferred to have gone on in a light-hearted way with our amusements and hobbies. But the bugle call came, and we have hung up the tennis racquet, we've fetched our laddie from school, we've put away his cap, and we have glanced lovingly over his last report which said 'Excellent' – we've wrapped them all in a Union Jack.

The Narrator:–

Before returning to France in mid-August 1918, Wilfred Owen wrote a letter in which he angrily referred to (*the voice of Owen*) "stinking Leeds & Bradford war profiteers reading John Bull on Scarborough sands..." John Bull was the jingoistic journal published by Horatio Bottomley. His propaganda and one-man recruitment campaigns up and down the country reputedly made him £78,000. In the summer of 1917 Siegfried Sassoon threw away his Military Cross, although he still proudly wore the mauve and white ribbon on his tunic, along with three gold wound bars.

Sassoon:–

A bullet is cleaner than a whore,
and she is surely purer than the ladies
of the Active Service League
handing out white feathers.

We will remember their ignorance
of Ypres, Passchendaele, Mons,
at the going down of the sun.

Though pacified with solemn Elgar
we will remember Rosa Lewis,

who trained her little bitch to bite
young men not in uniform.

Honour and sacrifice are noble words,
used most often by those who pay
others to clean their dirty shoes.

The voice of Bottomley:–

THIS IS MORE THAN WAR, MATE –
IT'S A CALL TO THE HUMAN RACE!

Sassoon resumes:–

Life, to be sure, is nothing much to lose
on a pedestal in Trafalgar Square.
Always, the crowd bays loudest
for blood, broken glass, Barabbas.
Brave men and cowards share
the same dark hole in war.

VIII. Whom the Kings Saluted.

The Narrator:–

Brigadier-General L. J. Wyatt, GOC British Troops France and
Flanders 1920, and Director of the War Graves Commission, wrote to
the Daily Telegraph in September 1939 - remembering the First
World War on the eve of the Second.

Wyatt:–

I issued instructions that the body of a British soldier, which would
be impossible to identify, should be brought in from each of the four
main. battle areas – the Aisne, the Somme, Arras and Ypres,
November 7th 1920, and placed in the chapel of St. Pol…The four
bodies lay on stretchers, each covered by a Union Jack; in front of the
altar was the shell of the coffin which had been sent from England to
receive the remains…Next morning, carried by the pall-bearers who
were selected from NCOs of the British and Dominion troops, it was
placed on a French military wagon and taken to Boulogne Quay
where a British destroyer was waiting…Six barrels of earth from the
Ypres Salient were put on board to be placed in the tomb at
Westminster Abbey.

The Narrator:–

How did the Unknown Soldier die?
Smelling larkspur, chewing the cud,
attacking, retreating,
messing his pants or eating,
up to his armpits in mud?

Was he a Rupert Brooke hero
longing for war's cleansing thrill,
or just a poor Mick
ill-fed and half-sick,
his medicine a Number Nine Pill?

Was he cut down before Christmas?
Did he run out of blood in the dark?
Were his feet chewed by rats,
was his face flayed by gas?
Did he think that war was a lark?

Was he a long way from Tipperary?
Did he go to Heaven or Arras?
Were his home fires kept burning,
did he freeze to death yearning
for crumpet and comfort in Paris?

Was he praying for a cushy,
or just trying to do his job?
Did he soften his boots with whiskey,
or knock it back like a rummy?
Did he believe in Haig or in God?

Did he drown in ten feet of water?
Was his skull caved in by a dud?
Did he relish the slaughter,
did his guts turn to water,
was he scared by the sight of his blood?

Was he blown to bits by the British,
or mistakenly gassed by the French?
Who can prove that he fell
by bullet, bayonet or shell
that came from a German trench?

Did he have VD? Was he lonely?
Could he read, did he write, was he queer?
Did he cheat, did he lie,
did he know how to die?
Was he shot at the Front or the rear?

Was he a Pal or a conscript?
Did he join because of the money?
Was he bonkers or bolshie,
did he try going conchie,
did he even believe in his country?

Siegfried Sassoon:–

As the Last Post blows in the morning
when the Book of Remembrance is read,
let this thought work its way to the surface
like shrapnel inside your head.
As you salute the Unknown Soldier
and murmur a prayer of regret,
just who do you choose to remember
and who do you choose to forget?

The Narrator:–

In February 1993, Britain's then-Prime Minister John Major
explained why a posthumous pardon for the 307 men shot at dawn
was not practicable. "We cannot rewrite history by substituting our
latter-day judgement for that of contemporaries, whatever we might
like to think. With the passage of time attitudes and values change."
Two years later, however, on the eve of the fiftieth anniversary of VJ
Day, Britain sought an apology from Japan for atrocities committed
by Japanese troops between December 1941 and August 1945 – Pearl
Harbour and Hiroshima. And on Good Friday, 1998, the British and
Irish Governments, supported by America and the European Union,
got a peace agreement for Northern Ireland, an agreement which
called for a substantial change of attitudes and values.

IX. Apologies Are All the Rage.

Lily MacDonald:–

Apologies are all the rage,
I know because I read it
printed on a broadsheet page.
Leave sleeping dogs where they lie.
Those three hundred men of grey
were hardly Spartans at Thermopylae.
Why disturb the dust of a bygone age?

The generals who won their spurs
with sword and pistol in bush and veldt
did not understand the language
of Maxim's fast-talking bullet belt.
Why dig up dead men's judgements
in the light of a different day?
Apologies are all the rage.

The works of soldier-poets
should teach each generation to heed
the harrowing pity of battle -
providing they can read.
Only time can turn back the clock,
we can only turn over the page...

Apologies are all the rage.

Acknowledgements

Half-a-dozen lines of Remembrance Sunday,
and the titles of all the poems except Apologies Are All the Rage,
were taken from poems published during the Great War which may
be found in Robert Giddings' book The War Poets.
These poems include Laurence Binyon's For the Fallen;
Rupert Brooke'sThe Soldier; Isaac Rosenberg's Dead Man's Dump;
Walter De La Mare's Happy England;
Wilfred Owen's The Send Off, and Mental Cases;
Winifred Letts' The Deserter;
and Siegfried Sassoon's Repression of War Experience.
Prose quotations are from Goodbye to All That, by Robert Graves,
and
Lyn Macdonald's Voices and Images of the Great War.
Other sources include: Dominic Hibberd's biography,
Wilfred Owen: The Last Year;
The Social History of the Machine Gun, by John Ellis;
John Keegan's The Face of Battle;
and Jon Stallworthy's biography, Wilfred Owen.
Information was also taken from stories in the following
newspapers:Yorkshire on Sunday; the Keighley News;
the Bradford Daily Telegraph; and the Telegraph & Argus.
Thanks are due to the Commonwealth War Graves Commission;
Keighley historian Alan Smith;
Dr Charles Vise at Bradford Royal Infirmary;
Mr Chris Hafford for invaluable factual information;
Barry MacSweeney for ideas and enthusiasm;
Ray Shilling, as always, for the machinery;
and War Poets Assistant at Napier University Isobel Liddle
whose hand-written notes and photostats greatly helped me with
this work's central section, Expression of War Experience.

Finally, this poem is dedicated to the
memory of my dear friend and fatherly encourager
Roger Suddards CBE;
without his insistence it would not
have been written.

10. TRIUMPH OF THE WILL

1. Leni and Herr Wolf

Leni Riefenstahl was born in 1902
to middle-class Germans; evidently well-to-do,
for while Europe danced its Dance of Death
Leni learned to pas-de-deux and pirouette;
the fall of Imperial Hohenzollerns
did not deprive her of sausage or Stollen.
In the hungry Twenties she caught her breath:
from ballerina to silent movie star
was but a step she took without regret.
Despite Versailles and the Wall Street Crash
Germany was on the march and so was Leni.
She played the part of ice maiden in distress
to good effect; but deep down in her ardent heart
she longed to dictate her destiny and direct.
Then came the Thirties, the Brownshirts,
and one man who, unlike Max Reinhardt,
seemed to detect as though by intuition
Leni Riefenstahl's secret ambition,
a man whose judgement she could respect.

I JUST WANT YOU
TO MAKE PICTURES FOR ME
JUST ABOUT ME
AND THE MOVEMENT.

The sky is as blue
as the Reich Chancellor's eye,
as blue as the irises of Mengele twins.
She has come down from her Tyrolean eyrie,
its hanging baskets, balconies
and Obersalzburg peaks,
                              Leni Riefenstahl
ninety, blonde and feisty.
Trim as a trip-wire, cute as a cat,
her mouth slits like Nancy Reagan's
when she smiles on camera.

Green Peace recluse, Maldives memshab.
Under the filmy substance of the Indian Ocean
silver tip, white tip, and grey reef sharks
flicker in and out the middle distance:
nightmares, memories. She tempts them,
the deep's dead-eyed führers,
to eat out of her hand.
Hitler, disposed to take a chance,
gave Leni Riefenstahl carte-blanche.
Her strategems included tantrums and tears,
but she made him three movies in five years.
Of these the one which to this day still
provokes controversy is Triumph of the Will.
Artistic documentary or artful propaganda:
warm advocates and testy critics seek
to justify conflicting arguments
using the same examples of her technique.

Her lens enlarges.
Each frame-filling face
shines with iron discipline
and Blood Banner obedience.
This National Socialist carapace
has the chiselled texture
of unflinching granite.
Hard Harz Mountain eyes
defy mere mutability.
She shoots each eager recruit
larger than life-size:
Germany's Rushmore sculptures.
Only time-lapsed clouds
disturb the stillness
with stormy movement.

2: Leni and Goebbels

Hobbling lothario Joseph Goebbels,
Minister of Culture and Propaganda,
liked nothing better than viewing
popular Hollywood movies at Lanke.
Behind the electric tinted-windows
who cared if Jews owned most of the studios.

Perhaps Leni resisted the Minister's
strong weakness for actresses,
what the party preached was pure and good.
Riefenstahl was the very antithesis
of the ideal of compliant womanhood.

If only David O. Selznick or Walt Disney
had worked for me! Gone with the Wind,
Snow White and the Seven Dwarfs –
that's what you call real propaganda.

Entertainment is best, I told Hitler:
don't write darling Leni a blank cheque.
Spoilt bitch thought our job was to bankroll
her ambition to outdo D.W. Griffith.

I told her: propaganda's what you do for love,
art is what you do for money.
I goaded Göring, but the fat emperor
only laughed. Who can sit still, truthfully,

through Triumph of the Will?
Those endless columns of marching men
shouldering shovels for the Reich!
Hitler, of course, was terribly impressed.

I thought each Wagnerian sequence trite,
but made sure I applauded louder than the rest.
Shirtless he-men cheerfully tossing logs
first thing in the morning – in September!

Clark Gable or Donald Duck would have done
the party's public image a power of good.
I told Speer: propaganda should be fun!
They do these things much better in Hollywood.

3: Sublimation of the Self

Does not your heart beat faster
when massed ranks move in unison?
They are like waves, like forest boughs.
Though your conscience says no,

does not your heart beat faster
as the earth shakes at this mass communion,
the union of separate parts?
Your heart says yes
though your conscience says no.
Obey your heart!
Renounce all volition,
let go, let go.

Cleanse me, rid me of myself,
blitz the superfluities.
Beat out the rhythm of my separateness
until I become the drum whose sound
cannot be distinguished from all the rest.

4: Conscience is a Jewish Invention

His Junkers makes the sign of the Cross
on the Brothers Grimm gables.
Hitler is not hidden, unlike God
his black crucifix is crooked.

The Führer seems to float
through his adoring domain in Hades.
Leni's cameras do not show him
standing on the seat of his Mercedes.

Born on April 20, 1889,
four days after Charlie Chaplin,
Germany's great dictator
has come a long way for an Ariean.

Vienna's dirty long-haired tramp,
impeccably smart and remarkably clean,
has come a long way from Stumpergasse,
the hostel financed by Epsteins.

Jews bought his painted picture postcards,
without them he would have been finished.
In these picturesque urban panoramas
the human figure is diminished.

The wheels of his bullet-proof chariot
crush the bouquets that Nurembergers,
shot in ecstatic close-up, throw
in the path of Germany's Nero.

5: In Concert

WE WILL
WE WILL ROCK YOU

    JUDENRAUS
    JUDENRAUS

WE WILL
WE WILL ROCK YOU

    JUDENRAUS
    JUDENRAUS

WE WILL
WE WILL ROCK YOU.

Thirteen hundred feet long and eighty wide,
Hitler's stage dwarfs Bayreuth's,
a proper platform to magnify
the little corporal, Braunau's cowboy.
Big as a North Sea oil rig, draped in Muslim black like the Kaaba.
Radio towers fifty feet high, red lights winking like satellites.
Twenty-four video screens. A million watts of pulsing
multi-media mega-myth wish-fulfilment. *WE WILL*
WE WILL ROCK YOU.

One hundred and thirty anti-aircraft lights
pour four miles upwards a Doric column of purest white:
Twentieth Century Fox in Nuremberg.
Forearms folded juttingly across his chest-
the pose in the choir-school photograph –
he has dreamed of this moment since the age of ten.
Twenty-four drummer boys, all the same one, beat out a rhythm
on the video screens. Eighty thousand, willing to surrender, respond
as one to the little drummer boy, drumming up the come, drumming
up the come. Does not your heart beat faster, dancing in unison?
Uninhibited, massed ranks moving as one? Though your conscience
says no, your heart says yes, let go, let go, beat out the rhythm
of my separateness until I cannot be distinguished from all the rest.

Three hours at a stretch his arias rasp and soothe:
now loud, now soft, but always hoarse.
Heated up by hot Kleig lights intestinal gases
explode uncontrollably. Sweat stains his brown shirt
black. The libretto's sardonic, brutal, coarse.

They sent me to jail
for seeking a solution
back in 1923
the first German Revolution.
Ten years later
wheel's come full circle
I am the Führer
and Weimar's in the shit-hole.
SIEG HEIL
my Blood Banner brothers
SIEG HEIL

So many traitors
too many others.
Up against an obstacle
eliminate the mothers.
You can't make an omelette
without breaking eggs
you can't make a nation
without cracking heads.
SIEG HEIL
farewell to inflation
SIEG HEIL
one people one nation
SIEG HEIL

JUDENRAUS
JUDENRAUS
WE WILL
WE WILL ROCK YOU

Take a horse to water
but you can't make it drink
swab a pig in champagne
but you can't expunge the stink.
To all of our critics
from Bradford to Berlin

if you won't be a German
we'll bash your bloody skulls in
SIEG HEIL
SIEG HEIL
SIEG HEIL

Riefenstahl shoots him from the waist up
only – Germany's Elvis Presley.

WE WILL
WE WILL ROCK YOU
WE WILL
WE WILL ROCK YOU

DEMOCRACY IS HYPOCRISY
DEMOCRACY IS HYPOCRISY
STRENGTH THROUGH JOY
JOY THROUGH STRENGTH
FREEDOM IS A CANCER
FREEDOM IS A PLOY
WE WILL WE WILL ROCK YOU

And the little drummer boy
drumming up the come, drumming
up the come, though your conscience
says no your heart beats faster,
as the little boy's drum
beats away our differences
makes us all willing, makes us all one.

WE WILL
WE WILL ROCK YOU
WE WILL
WE WILL ROCK YOU.

6: Reality is What the Artist Edits

Holinshed's Chronicles at his elbow,
Shakespeare writes in his Bishopsgate lodgings.
Through the upstairs lattice
he can see Richard III's Crosby Place.
Betrayal is the essence of drama,
so he betrays the truth about Tricky Dicken
to validate a Tudor usurper.

7: Leni Triumphant

Stripped of her wet suit and mask,
Leni sits on the steps
of Speer's Hollywood set.
In high heels and stockings
effortlessly she reflects
on shutter-speeds, angles, lenses.
She faultlessly remembers
every bit of footage
her sixteen cameramen shot
that September. *Silver tip, white
tip, and grey reef sharks
flicker in and out the middle distance:
nightmares, memories, the deep's
dead-eyed führers.* That film
was a triumph of her will.
Six days of hell shooting,
six months in the dark cutting
cropping, splicing, doctoring
running reality backwards
through her projector.
But as to Hitler's politics
and problematic questions
of art and propaganda...
THEY DO NOT MIX!
She snarls at the camera.

8: Frederick the Great and Voltaire Debate Truth and Beauty

VOLTAIRE: Your Majesty, permit me to inquire
which of those two impostors you most admire?

FREDERICK: Beauty. (*He takes Voltaire by the crook of his arm*).
And you, Cher Maitre?

VOLTAIRE: (*He plucks a blossom from the orangery
and takes out his watch*). Truth (*he lies*),
Truth every time Your Majesty.

FREDERICK: Rousseau believes that beauty is higher,
ennobling Man's moral nature.
Beauty separates us from the beasts.

VOLTAIRE: Ah, Rousseau, Jean-Jacques, the Swiss!
(*Voltaire sighs. He misses his garden at Ferney:
the chestnuts, the avenue of beeches
nurtured so cleverly that lords and ladies
must bow pomaded perukes to walk under it:
thus conquerors stoop to gardeners*).
A weeping moralist, a royalist republican
rooted in contradiction and dilemma,
as well as a congenital inability
to discipline either his pen or his prick.

FREDERICK: Not the only man of letters
of the Eighteenth Century, I think,
at the mercy of his desire
to spill the world with seed and ink!

VOLTAIRE: This noble savage, whom monarchs defend,
would remain unmoved by the thought
of thirty thousand men bleeding
on the field of battle. But should a child
take a tumble and scratch so much
as a flea-bite, Rousseau's up half the night
sobbing before a glass. Suffering humanity!
This philosophic gentleman sired
five bastards by a barmaid
philosophy would not let him marry.

Unwilling to be distracted
from ennobling Mankind, he
despatched each brat
to the Sisters of Charity.

FREDERICK: You doubt the fellow's sincerity?

VOLTAIRE   I do not doubt the tears in his nose
when he orphaned his offspring.
It's not his gravity I question
but his philosophy. Rousseau's
a sentimentalist, and sentimentalists
most easily mistake passion
for virtue; they cannot comprehend
why others do not behave as they do.
Politically they are dangerous,
especially when they rhapsodise
original innocence.
There is no greater treason
than the treason of the senses.

FREDERICK: Rousseau may be a fool or a rogue,
more suited to poetry than prose
Voltaire, but may not the blind apprehend
phenomena the sighted cannot see?
We live in a state of paradox:
Nature uplifts and humbles simultaneously.
Without beauty, what you are pleased
to traduce as treason, what crimes
would Man not commit in the name of Reason?

VOLTAIRE: Does Your Majesty then rule
in a state of grace or desperation?
Paradox! Spare a poor Frenchman
your Prussian equivocation.
There is no more natural morality
in this blossom than in Versailles,
a woman's tits, or this landscape.
Were this not so murder would be exclusive
to slums and dunghills; but, as we know,
wars are planned in palaces
and terrible things are done in beautiful places.

And yet, according to Rousseau,
kings and peasants are born free
and equally well-disposed towards Mankind.
In years to come men will rue the night
Rousseau senior had that fatal erection.
The act of love is beautiful,
every fuck's an immaculate conception;
but pity the poor world
that must bear the consequences.

9: A Spring Afternoon at Ravensbruck

Butlin's has no better site
than this secluded clearing,
hidden by cool uplifting pines.
The lake, as neutral as Geneva,
is as peaceful and pastoral
as an Eighteenth Century landscape.

Against humanity
it's best to commit crimes
in beauty spots.
                    Later,
on spring afternoons like this one,
sight-seers will come along
to look through viewfinders for shots
and declare:
                    What unkind heart
could flourish here?

                    At Ravensbruck
the very brightness of the grass
inspires the soul with harmony.
You can smell wild flowers
but not the fear
                    which went up in smoke.

High above the crematorium,
as spick and span as a bakery,
a cuckoo might bring to mind
The Creation, or even
Mozart's Requiem.

Violette Szabo,
the women of Lidice,
saw their last blue sky here.

Death in the mass
is abstract, a statistic
revisionist historians dispute.

On spring afternoons at Ravensbruck
think of one death only,
singular and absolute.

10: Smoke (In memory of Ellen Dorothy Wade Greenhalf)

The scent of death in summer is sweet.
In death as in life
I am hot and out of place.
My wedding clothes
cling oppressively.
The black road wavers
in August heat.

It looks like a branch line
waiting-room,
a terminus in the sticks,
where sleepers wait
                        for trains
to whistle them awake.
Among his roses
a man scatters ashes
he has knocked from the grate.
Forgotten confetti
falls from my pocket
as we make for the gates.

Into the simple air
a single column of smoke
unravels its blue farewell
and, like a prayer,
begins the journey to Heaven.

11: Leute Brennen Sehr Gut, Herr Lanzmann

Treblinka's sixteen barbers:
Riefenstahl's sixteen cameramen.
Human hair made comfortable shoes
for North Atlantic U-boat crews.

Haftlinge played football
while Musselmen were chosen
to blister the chimney's lips
before the final whistle.

From a distance
of five kilometres
advancing British soldiers
could smell Belsen.

12: Birthday Present

Five days before Hitler's
fifty-sixth and final birthday,
they pushed the gates open.
She lay on the ground,
a sack of broken candles.
Clustered round her,
like moths around a flame,
clumsy squaddies from mill-towns.
They offered her water,
she asked for a flower,
to smell something sweeter
something to help her remember
the difference between Heaven
and where she was.
But there were no flowers
for this girl of sixteen.
She died in the spring,
on the day of liberation,
in her hands a dusty dandelion:
the only thing of beauty
given her by a man.

13: In Concert II

LOTS OF WOMEN
ARE ATTRACTED TO ME
BECAUSE I AM UNMARRIED.

Either in art or in death
love's inadequacies are resolved.
Adolf Hitler: Ill for Death.
Artist of the brazen glance
whose gift was gas.
His paintbrush bristles
on his upper lip.
Centre-stage Nero's fingers
strangle, crush and grip.

Infinity of faces
expectant in the lights
I've got a proposition
in Nuremberg tonight
send the Yids to Madagascar
take by force what's ours by right
and for the bastards who betray us
eternal fog and night
SIEG HEIL
my bold kamaraden
SIEG HEIL
don't apologise or pardon
SIEG HEIL

WE WILL
WE WILL ROCK YOU

14: Love Song for 93,000 Women

Here's to Odette and Violette,
and to all the women I never knew
who loved men who loved them;
whose moment of truth
fell upon them in Gestapo cellar
SS clearing or beneath a sky
of unbelievable blue;
whose children were orphaned or unborn.

Remember those who took the steps
to save us following them
thereafter. Although the world turns
and all the rest forget, I will
think of them winter and summer,
for love is valid in retrospect.
Loving one I love them all,
my Dandelion Girl, and Violette.

In her eyes there are secret places
inhabited by faces she never knew.
She looks at me and sometimes I see them,
and in my eyes she sees them too.
Lidice's mothers and daughters
and others murdered before her birth;
loving her they are not forgotten,
they stream like hair above the earth.

15: Leni and Lodz

Over Piedmont alpine thunderclouds
roll eastwards like boxcars.
Rain beats its fists on the roofs of Turin.
The sky opens for Primo Levi, whose scars
once again burst and bleed within.
Dante, in his vision of Hell,
required the services of Virgil;
so I have brought back 174517
to question Leni Riefenstahl.

What was it made you cry at Lodz?
Shooting non-persons is merely matter-of-fact:
one second they live, another they do not.
Were those killers you caught in the act
the young you filmed six years before, framed
against heroic skies? Were those blue-eyed kids
the same ones grinning from black trains
en route to Poland to slaughter Yids?

When Germany bloomed with yellow stars
and the Reich's wise men burned the books,
smoke perhaps blinded you to the meaning
of those fires, the hatred in people's looks.
Obscured by the banner of the crooked cross,
what truth conspired to make you transfigure
Germany's pathological boss,
who stamped his boots in Brownshirt viscera?

When art renounces ethics connoisseurs
of concertos, nocturnes and sonatas
happily strangle men with piano wire.
It is possible to love cantatas
and mastermind the Final Solution.
Violin-playing Heydrich did his duty.
Auschwitz was merely the manifestation
of the pursuit of ultimate beauty.

Yeats worried belatedly in later life
a play of his had inspired men to murder.
Is your conscience troubled by Macbeth's knife?
Perhaps those pyres made your eyes water.
You say you did not know what Hitler was,
even though Krystallnacht preceded Lodz.
Tell me, you who are waiting to die,
I'd like to know, what it was that made you cry.

PROPAGANDA, ONLY PROPAGANDA IS NECESSARY:
THERE IS NO END OF STUPID PEOPLE.

16: Letter from the BNP

About the holocaust he sites piles of shoes
and hair as "proof" of mass extermination.
There is a simpler explaination.
Typhus was a big problem in those areas,
to delouse somebody you had to remove
their clothes and hair.
Germans accepted repatriation,
the often talked of final solution.
Let's have the facts about the Holohoax.
People like Spielberg will be seen as profiteers
on the Second European Brothers' War,

sob stories made up to make us,
the European youth, feel guilty.
We've nothing to be guilty of.
We haven't managed to stop the rot,
but we're working on it.

17: Uncovering a War Criminal

The old man accused of terrible crimes
was just a name to me. I had not seen
this culprit or victim of abnormal times
until they showed his photograph on screen.
They claimed it was him, an incriminating
Iron Cross ribbon on his battledress.
He had, they said, sought to save his skin
while unarmed villagers with no redress
were mown down among their crops.
He wore a disarming cardigan,
a crucifix hung below a modest clock.
Big hands on short wrists, the fingers thick
like those of a butcher or engineer.
They said he had concealed the part he played
for more than forty years, had lived a lie
religiously – although he often prayed.
He said war's bad luck had put the guns
into the hands of men honed for killing;
what could he do, what would they have done?
Dissent meant death. They seemed to be willing,
it would not suit their purpose to anger him
and be turned away. The crew had a film to shoot.
They too, it seems, had orders to obey.

18: The Ghost of Brecht Whispers a Warning

When the shit of fear is running down your legs
don't stand on ceremony, unless for a bit more air.
Truly, the meek shall inherit the earth –
but only when they're good and dead.

Past forty a man gets short of breath
but breathes more easily, prepared
to believe the apocalypse has passed
his lintel, that he's been spared.
He mistakes the right as his,

having survived the years of exile
where he earned his daily bread.
When the good years came he smiled:
time for endless chess and in summer
the legs of pretty women to admire.

Then out of the blue like lightning –
offensives are launched in spring and summer –
shaved impenitential deaths heads
cordon-off the town and take away the men,
of whom nothing more is heard.

When enough territory has been stolen
the deaths heads turn into butterflies,
hawks become doves. Blessed are the peace-makers.
But below the horizon of their lies
suffering's converted into acres.

Exhort a man without a face to face the future:
assure a woman without a womb she's reborn:
explain to the son why you butchered his father,
then tell me what you know of grief.

19: The Girl in the Red Cardigan

She swings like a telephone
dropped in a hurry. First right,
then left, oscillating
against the world's turning;
balanced by stiff arms,
dancing her slow dance alone.

How old did they say? Twenty,
making her ten a decade ago
when artists formed a human chain,
and Bob and Midge and Bono
said there was no need to be afraid
in a world of plenty.

She hanged herself in a safe place,
her noose torn from a UN sheet.
No hope in her heart, no shoes
on her feet, and no one to
close her swollen eyes.
In death they gave her the space.

Behind my back I hear the man
talk to pictures which ten years ago
shamed the world into action.
In front of me, head on one side
as though asking a question,
the girl in the red cardigan.

Toes turned shyly inward,
a girl on her first big date.
The tree from which she suspended
her belief blooms: she is the fruit
this summer. No tears in her eyes
now her lonely dance has ended.

Poets will write her poems for sure,
and white candles will be lit
at rock concerts and vigils.
When the worst is over such things
make uplifting subjects for songs,
and award-winning literature.

**Saturday, July 15, 1995 -
the tenth anniversary of Live Aid.**

11. From **BERLIN**

More Coffee, More Cordial

I wasn't expecting a kiss,
but suddenly she filled my hands
with guidebooks, maps,
crashed into first
and screeched off
towards Marx-Engels Platz.

Turning the corner
of the Maxim Gorky Theatre,
I rehearse each act of the morning.
She eyed me sideways,
as though I did not belong.
Far from being her deus ex machina
I was a spanner in the works.

I'll change your life
and other ex cathedra pronouncements
return to blame my face.
Betrayed herself,
she turned me into the traitor.

At the Checkpoint Charlie Cafe
coffee and cordial bitte.
The girl behind the counter
has long black hair.
Bon appetit, she says,
I could kiss her.

Sugar dissolves like self-assurance.
Jesus, sweeten my imagination.
Is there a sign on my forehead,
a star on my coat?
Bite tongue, swallow pride, eat words.
Fragments stick in my throat.

More coffee, more cordial bitte.
A friend is an enemy
who has not yet betrayed you.

You Need Good Shoes on the Unter Den Linden

Mine are Saxone
and make no noise.
They wouldn't dare
in the wake of Bismarck,
Frederick the Great,
and Hitler's boot-boys.

The Brandenburg Gate
is a knuckleduster.
History's triumphal march
makes my feet ache.
I check my teeth
on the Tiergarten –
green parade ground
made for stomping in unison.

Foreign souls prefer
anonymity, it's safer.
You couldn't mistake me
for one of those
Economic Refugees -
they all wear trainers.
My shoes are black,
silent and shiny

like Jesse Owens.

Autobahn

We're driving
out of our minds
along Autobahn 96
Berlin to Leipzig.
The single wiper
slashes an arc
the way ahead
uncertain.
Yves Montand
celebrates the Seine,
Paris, love.

She puts her foot down,
speed diminishes distance
but not the pain.

A customs post
unmanned, no use,
sick trees. No respite
just Autobahn 96
pock-marked
and pot-holed
all the way to Dresden,
the way ahead
uncertain.

She loads
another cassette.
Another cloud
unloads its cargo.
Marlene Dietrich,
fallen angel
laughing at love again,
razor in her stocking.
The single wiper
slashes an arc.
Distance diminishes
but not the pain.

The Dog's Not Laughing

Amid the grubby grandeur of a Leipzig square
Goethe sniffs on a pedestal.
Faust's troubled author
smells trouble in the air.
Bad odour blowing from the Oder-Neisse.

Out of a cloud of photographers
Chancellor Kohl – Mephistopheles – appears
shooting spotlessly white cuffs
from a suit of midnight blue,
no tricks up there.

Two old men quarrel,
impatient to hear his prognosis.
One nation with two hearts:
will it survive and prosper
or tear itself apart?

Kohl descends the hospital steps,
scribbles his signature,
waves, then ducks into the rear
of the awaiting Merc,
the audience cheers.
Blue flashes, sirens shrieking,
the old devil disappears.

Well, what do you think?
Goethe says to a passing Alsatian.
It cocks a leg. A pigeon
flying East to West replies,
Johann, the dog's not laughing.

From the Boulevard Café
*Old East German bank-notes weighing 2,000 tonnes are being
stored in 131,000 sacks in a disused mine. Germany is apparently
eagerly awaiting the outcome of a Bank of England test to see if
they can be turned into compost.* The Guardian, 8-11-91.

MARX, ENGELS, LENIN
                                farewell:
no more free ads.

BMW posters fill windows
of the tram depot.
Trusting Hands and Pepsi-Cola
are taking over.
Instead of Communism
                                Clearasil.
Just rub it in
for half-a-century.
Politicophotosynthesis:
Germany, like the language,
is built on compound structures.
Plants open and close mysteriously.

Forty-six years to the day
Hitler shot himself in the head,
the Trabant is given the bullet.
Soon only Bratwurst will be
the East's sole manufacture.
Anything is soup
if a pinch of salt is added.
Old ideas are easier to swallow
reheated: The Deutsche Alternative.

More to sell
but who can buy?
Paradise regained
promises to be hell.

Mekong eyes smoulder
on footbridges
above party badges
and unsold cigarettes.

Bulgarians and Yugoslavs
importune shoppers
to bet on Lady Luck,
one eye on the coppers.

A bearded German
sings alone
The Green Green
Grass of Home.

Round and round
the Rathaus square
a man pounds out his anguish
on a drum. Walled up
for fifty years,
men lose their jobs
and then their minds.
Gott Allein Die Ehre
says the motto in goldleaf
gothic on the hospital tower.
Have patience would be better.

In the brown vestibule
of the International Hotel
we sit in the Boulevard Café.
The day is ending
with coffee black.

Outside in the street
boys bounce balloons
between chrome wheels
of swish saloons.
He whose bright idea
does not burst
first, he, I guess
has won.

Some are born lucky;
others have it thrust upon them.
The rest are ruled
by resentment.

Darkness descends.
Above the chassis of the GDR
the symbol of Mercedes-Benz.

Memorabilia

I bought Winnetou, volumes one and two,
turgid epic of the Golden West
by Karl May (1842-1912),
Hitler's lifelong favourite writer.

West of Brandenburg Gate
copper-skinned men touted tourists,
offering cold warrior insignia:
tin stars, pistols,
and other law and order symbols.

Nine foot chunks of the Iron Curtain,
100,000 dollars a slab,
make decorative artefacts
on crewcut college lawns
in Fulton, Missouri.

Red Army memorabilia
in the state of Jesse James.

Bullet holes in the Reichstag
mark the place of the final shoot-out.
The gaps in Berlin's memory
plugged and patched with plaster.

Past repairing, black bootheels
of Soviet soldiers.
Knees akimbo they walked
like Walter Brennan in Red River.
Empty holsters slapped
mustard-coloured pants.
Marshalling towns
they once cleaned-up
but never did belong to.

Redmen hunched over smoking bottles,
shooting the breeze outside
run-down clapboard houses,
unpainted, peeling gables.
Unwanted extras, not box office,
neither warriors nor heroes.
Back in West Berlin,
queues for Dances with Wolves
do not care to remember.

Hang-gliding for Beginners

*East Germany's old communists believed that everyone who wanted
to fly, wanted to fly West, so they banned most amateur aeronautics.
Now the restrictions have gone, the country is taking wing.*
The Independent on Sunday, 11-3-90.

Tonight we leave the Las Vegas
lights of West Berlin.
Her Peugeot tumbrils
over strasses double-parked
with Wartburgs and Trabis.
They hog gutters
outside pork and herring
apartment blocks –

opera-balconied backwaters
lit by sixty watts.

An inaudible melody –
piano, fiddle, accordion –
lingers on stone stairs
Mozart or Einstein
might have known.
Cabbagewater corridors
wide enough for two
armed men to drag
a third. She feels
at home here:
West of Tempelhof
despair is more authentic.
Something in her
longs to languish
in this cold water quarter,
a soul in anguish.
Suffering is timeless,
she longs to suffer.

Rich bastards with bathrooms
stay out of hot water.
It is unbecoming,
a sign of bad faith,
to crave high ceilings
and decent plumbing.
Elevated feelings
belong in hovels.
She'd swap her central heating
for a stove in the corner,
the type with tiles
in Russian novels.
I blame Jean-Paul Sartre.

Flaubert, I tell her,
was a bourgeois.
Emile Zola
wore frocked coats,
kept servants and
Second Empire furniture.
Who cares?

Were I an entrepreneur
I'd build a replica of the Wall,
charge anguished intellectuals
a punishing figure
for crash courses
in the art of survival –
hang-gliding for beginners.

Goodbye To the Past

A Neo-Nazi had died of AIDS.
Stefan fetched a bottle of red
and we drank one another's health.
She met him in a bar of The Star Hotel.
He showed us his brand new sofa,
at night it doubled as his bed.

I watched them talking together,
sometimes in German, sometimes French -
the advantage of languages.
I pictured them walking together
arm-in-arm in Charlottenberg.
There's a sign at Checkpoint Charlie,
only yards away from the border -
of the wire, the Wall, the security
there is no evidence, just the sign
in English, German, Russian and French.
Where something begins it also ends.

Along Oranienbergerstrasse
it is possible to purchase a piece
of Jewish ass, Stefan laughed:
sex always sells. Before the fall
it could only be bought in hotels
selected and sanctioned by
a party organ. Now, out in the open,
abortion-gaunt girls kiss goodbye to the past.

You Don't Know What Love Is

It's seventeen below in Warsaw,
olive oil freezes in the bottle.
I'm sitting in her Berlin apartment,
spring, in a vase dead flowers -
I'll replace them - she's in bed,
leaving me on the floor
with Raymond Carver's poems
she brought back from Dublin.

Red light on her answer machine
glows like a last cigarette.
A man leaves a message in French
I do not understand. Carver
remembers the night Charles Bukowski,
half-crazed, drunk probably,
creamed a roomful of sophomores:
You don't know what love is!
She shared my mail with an American,
they sat together on this floor.
She opened her arms and let him in.

At the crossroads between the heart
and that place below the belt
where love and treachery start,
each has his own Checkpoint Charlie.
There's snow in Berlin,
in Warsaw it's seventeen below;
olive oil freezes and I need someone
with the bottle to show me what love is.

12. From **THE LUCY POEMS**

She Acts Upon Me Like a Force of Nature

She acts upon me like a force of nature,
her blouse the colour of crocuses.
In the weak light of her Irish Geordie eyes
wild daffodils, frightened irises.
No sense of time but a notion of eternity.
She is lost and found, she is the sound
of Uillean pipes above Lough Swilly.
Her nights are cold apartments,
candlelit basements in foreign cities,
plunging necklines, Senegalese reggae.
Her body is a cello played by Jacqueline Du Pré.
Her central nervous system is a railway map
from Manchester to Warsaw.
Daughter of the Tyne, sister of the Irwell.
woman of Isis and the Vltava.
Her heart, which belongs to nobody,
is the Free Trade Hall in November.
Her happiness is a lamplit embankment,
rain on a starry skylight below Hradčany.
She is October sunlight pouring through
forty-four windows of the Hockney Gallery.
Mistress of the hummed song and brassy fanfare,
waif of the veil, silver-earringed gypsy,
my lovely American Asphodel lily.

Daughter of Compassion, Reason and Deceit

Daughter of compassion, reason and deceit,
bewitches me with the mere movement
of her lips, which I have never kissed,
tasting of Bulgarian Cabernèt Sauvignon.
Modigliani model in a Prussian Green cardigan,
folding her limbs between the wings of an armchair,
head bowed in gaslit-flickering darkness,
left hand pushing back her falling hair.
At the Curlew Café she boldly wore
black leotard, leggings, jacket and boots:
a cross between Max Wall and a terrorist,
yet too shy to be first through the door.

Now she bustles busily about
in her crumpled white Narodnik shirt,
a repressed actress or school-teacher –
Nina, Irina – head bowed by the weight
of thick-lensed spectacles.
Neither cruel nor kind, not wanting to know,
preoccupied, working for the greater good,
but dying to escape to Moscow.

She Never Lay Under My Heart

She never lay under my heart.
Her tongue's tip
did not slit my mouth.
My fingertips never traced
the warm indent of her hips.
Her breasts gave me
neither succour nor pleasure.
She would not let me soothe her
tenseness with my big hands.
Her scarred knee did not
embrace my back like a cello.
I did not play the fool for her,
the little boy or the man.

I fell in love
because of a song.
What is a song?

Snow's secret bitter impulse,
the heart's disappointed
desire to belong.

13. From CUT

Flashback

I've just come through the door on Shakespeare Street,
time to kill before the train
takes me back across the river.

The sky looks bad above Amen Corner,
on Pilgrim Street it's brighter
in blue-reflecting water.

Familiar red double-deckers
redolent of the sea.
The North Road ends in a door of green

and the beach beyond where I wrote her name.
Sea-window through which life roared
faintly. I loved her and she

I'm here, don't worry…
Winter landscape, her dark blue dress,
eyes I can neither close nor bless.

Sunset Boulevard

In the end writing alone,
Billy Wilder talking on television.
Out of the blue the telephone:
It's me, she says.

Once a year she calls,
won't give her number.
Maybe next time a woman will answer,
she says every year.
I tell her: *Watch Sunset Boulevard.*
She knows the ending, she says
I'm going to have sex instead.

At midnight I'm watching Gloria Swanson
while she's making love in bed.
William Holden dies facing the pool bottom.

My favourite movies are black and white.

Farewell, My Lovely

Coleridge wrote his Ode
to Dejection for Robert Mitchum,
who looks as though he's just flown in
from Kyoto, Seoul or Armageddon.
Hooded sardonic eyes
knife me inscrutably within
or, sometimes, simply don't give a damn.
Where is the passion and the life?
Hell, no use asking me buddy.
The mouth is emphatic
above his doubter's cloven chin.

Double Indemnity

Finally everything
comes down to insurance.
Raymond Chandler
slugs a final lunchtime martini.
Across the lot from Lucey's
the typewriter is waiting
at Paramount. Wilder
is waiting. Start
with the end,
Chandler thinks.
With the fastidious
self-confidence
of a lush,
he rises from the booth
like William Powell
and announces:
*In the beginning
was the dénouement.*

The Loud Lament of Fred C. Dobbs

Misfortune, they say, is character-forming.
Staying true to yourself, irrespective
of the slings and arrows aimed
at your heart's best hope,
sorts the men from the boys.

What they really mean is,
there's always another sucker
waiting to be sapped.
Too much misfortune
makes you cultivate bad luck.
Life sucks is stating the obvious.
Every sucker, every sap, needs his day in the sun.
Do you ever wonder what happens to the mugs
who never seem to get one?

On the Waterfront

When I'm no longer box-office,
when my lights are all punched out
and I'm lying, mitts crossed,
before the altar, don't nail me down
with speeches by those who could have,
those who should have helped
me think better of myself.
Don't let them praise me or nominate me,
don't let them tell one another
how much they're going to miss me.
Don't commission a biography,
just set up a projector, kill the lights,
and show them On the Waterfront.
Show them how I too tried
to be a stand up guy like Joey Doyle,
Kayo Dugan, and Father Barry.
Don't send them off with music
to satisfy their self-sealing hearts,
hit them hard between the eyes.
Show them I was a contender,
robbed of his chance.
Charley, make them remember.

Misfits I

More vulnerable than Marilyn Monroe,
Montgomery Clift, *acting*
as though a Master-Mix was up his ass,
said Brando. Gritty, put-upon
Jewish sonofabitch,
he didn't want anyone to know.

He almost steals Red River,
one of the Duke's finest.
And in the bombed-out rubble
of ruined Berlin
I am the urchin
for whom he searches.

He personified anxiety and anguish.
In the tenements of his eyes,
hallways of resentment
and sadness. He is the guy
pooled in bar-room shadow,
unable to get acquainted.

Misfits II

How could Joan Crawford be a five-star bitch
and yet elicit love and sympathy
as murdering Mildred Pierce?
I thought James Cagney was Cody Jarrett,
until I saw him sing and dance
in Yankee Doodle Dandy.

Lonely kids and those fallible to love
most easily fall for people
who act a part. Took me time to see
that artifice and Bogie were not the same,
though art is the final syllable
of his lip-twisted name.

Moral feelings seek for sympathy.
We are all cinematographers,
framing the set of circumstances
in which we picture reality.
Sometimes the true companions of the heart
are simply people who play a part.

Of Mice and Men

I should have killed her, I should've
taken from her what she took from me.
I gave her *The Best Years of Our Lives,*
she left me lies to suffer.
Humphrey Bogart or Clark Gable
would have handled it better.

Half of me is Lennie,
the harder half is George.
If you pass this way again
you may see him staring darkly
at the other in Rick's, rehearsing
the pain of the past at a corner table.
Humphrey Bogart or Clark Gable
would have handled it better.

Put me under the gaze
of the man with no eyes.
They had to shoot Cool Hand Luke,
McMurphy they had to lobotomise.
I deserve the asylum. Nurse Ratched's
squelching rubber soles, the stiff
white wings of her disapproving cap.
Too busy picturing myself as Shane,
ranging the crooked country
of lies, riding proud and lonesome
into technicoloured companionable sunsets.
But sunsets are cold. I couldn't see
over the next horizon. I should
have killed her, or she
should have finished me.

Love, I said, but what did I really know?
Sometimes you have to go for your guns,
shoot the words that kill and be prepared to go
unforgiven. Knowing men fight for their happiness,
she didn't believe I had the guts to make her suffer.
Humphrey Bogart or Clark Gable
would have handled it better.

White

She waited alone in the nave,
unlike brides on the day of marriage.
Tonight her bridal bed a grave,
the rolling earth her nuptial carriage.
From the long avenue in the dark church
we walk to the treeless cemetery.
Behind us fraudulent snow
erases the path as we go.

Midnight Cowboy

Shelley Winters
is Simone Signoret,
without her fatal tenderness.

Women have a weakness,
like moths to a flame,
for life's Joe Lamptons.

The black road follows me home
like Robert De Niro's
bundle of sorrow and remorse.

My heart sends out messages,
the red callbox at the end of the world
rings repeatedly.

Some way down the road
I might meet Sandy Dennis.
Or Jeanne Moreau.

Somewhere across the line
of Heaven's horizon,
red as the lips of Marilyn Monroe,

some lonely Juliette Binoche
or sad Irene Jacob
may be waiting.

Stars

Should we damn to hell the fate
that sentenced Audrey Hepburn,
the waif and gypsy of grace,
to die from cancer of the colon?

Should we lay waste every mourning wreath
and blow the smoke back in God's face
for plucking Judy Garland
undignified from life,
                              on the toilet?

Should we scream blue murder
because Jayne Mansfield,
whose figure eight tied men in knots,
lost her head in a car crash?

Should we seek a plea of mitigation
from whatever controlling fate
shapes destiny, a plea for Vivien Leigh
so fouled and fucked with self-hate?

In whatever shape or state
death takes us away
the best of what we are remains,
a semblance of eternity stays.

And so the stars will be brighter,
the seeming futility of our days
mitigated, our burdens
                              made lighter,
if only for the time it takes

to remember Audrey singing Moon River,
Judy flinging her young heart over
the rainbow, Jayne smiling,
and Vivien in silhouette
                              yearning for Tara.

FX: 2001

Jason and his Argonauts,
in crude pursuit of the Golden Fleece,
invoked the aid of Zeus's sister.
I could do with Hera or Ray Harryhausen,
a few special effects, a deity or two.

This life would try the patience
of saintly Robert Bresson,
immasculate Samson, Hercules,
let alone muscle-bound Steve Reeves.
Lend me the bicycle of Vittorio de Sica,

send me Stanley Kubrick or Gene Roddenberry.
Oh for the ineluctable logic of Dr Spock.
Dematerialise me Scotty, beam my particles
back to Saturn, or to Pluto,
but do not make me mortal again.

Mutiny on the Bounty

Hope, long-suffering Russians say,
is the last thing to die.
Life without hope is bad enough,
but living with it is tough.

Bligh is Apollo, Christian Dionysus:
two gods commanding the same
unquiet soul, struggling for supremacy
within the body of The Bounty.

Cape Horn's the shortest way to go
to Hell or Heaven – Davy Jones or Tahiti.
We're not here to gratify ourselves!
But why risk paradise for purgatory?

What good's a compass or a map
against two oceans, destiny and fate?
Our job's to serve and do our duty!
In God's name where's the joy in that?

Cast adrift on the irrational ocean,
unyielding Bligh gets his men to safety.
Christian and his fallen angels
reach Pitcairn and die in anonymity.

Victor

Whenever I swat a bat-like moth
or smack an irritating fly,
I thank Christ I'm not a Buddhist.
That vampirish thing whirring
outside in the night,
or sleeping on the ceiling,
might be Rudolf Valentino,
Sydney Greenstreet,
or the late Victor Buono.

Were I inclined to believe
that souls transmigrate,
Victor would be Napoleon
on St Helena, or Oliver Hardy.
The Hermann Göring
of Hollywood – *The Strangler,*
The Mad Butcher –
sinister but disarmingly cute
in his buttoned-up shirt.
Enough material in his suit
to wrap a Japanese Zero.

He was the fat man women
feel sorry for, until
his mamma's boy fingers
unforgivingly pincered their throat.
Victor, emperor of serial killers,
might have started out as Nero.

When Did They Ever Let You Down?

When did they ever let you down?
John Ireland and Walter Huston,
wardrobe-sized Ward Bond,
gabby Walter Brennan:
regular guys you could depend upon
between Red River and Rio Grande.

Let's hear it for Chill Wills,
Slim Pickens and dependable
William Bendix; Lee Marvin and Audie
Murphy (authentic war heroes
with Purple Hearts and bad dreams);
Martin Balsam and Woody Strode,

and under-rated Robert Ryan –
Saddam Hussein without the beret.
Poles opposed to the tin tsar
plastered Poland with posters
of Gary Cooper in High Noon.
What do you think they did that for?

Trading Places

Praise be to Alex Haley,
                         alias Kunta Kinte,
for inventing spurious African
                                 antecedents.
The credulous, the self-righteous
brothers - he fooled 'em good,
shafted a generation
                     and made a mint.

Why hobble yourself with orthopaedic roots?
Charlton Heston started out
in No Man's Land
                (North Chicago).
Moses did not make it across the Jordan.

My first hero was world-roaming Alexander,
whose home was anywhere but his own.
He set out a Greek and became a Persian.

To unravel the truth about Ireland
Joyce had to slip the umbilical
that bound him to the preconceptions
of his time-confounded race.

Trieste, Rome, Zurich, Paris -
Europe gave birth to Bloom.
To his gas-lit, gaseous, gasbag culture
Joyce brought The Volta,

                    Dublin's first cinema.

To those who proclaim nothing lasting or of beauty grows
unless nurtured by soil of native places,
throw the following names, Kunta,

                 in their faces:-
George and Ira Gershwin,

           Kirk Douglas,
Billy Wilder, John Ford,

          Danny Kaye,
Dmitri Tiomkin,

        Frank Sinatra,
all the Hollywood moguls,
not forgetting Miklos Rosza.

Uprooted, transplanted, or born into an alien culture
every one. Behind every starry-eyed American
the eyes of an exiled generation.
Forget East of Eden and James Dean
(except in Giant), remember Steve

               (part Italian)

                  McQueen.

My good friend Ernest, born poor in Bolton,
plays Bartok with the heart

           of an émigré Slav.
Where we are born is a point of departure.
The fittest who survive the races

          and thrive
are those more adept at trading places.

Buttons

As England crossed the border of the Nineteen Fifties
the cinemascopic New Frontier was lit up
by the sea-blue eyes of Jeffrey Hunter,
Hollywood's first full-facial Jesus.
In close-up his unflinching
Galilean gaze was truly a wonder,

steadier than unblinking Kennedy's.
But I was more mesmerised by the sight
of my first buttoned-down collar shirt,
worn by Tab Hunter or another
of those college campus pin-ups,
who owned convertibles and thin ties.

To kids like me, itching in thick vests
and embarrassing three-quarter length pants,
these guys were as far out as Martians.
How could a rural rube like Khrushchev,
cunning hard-headed bluffer though he was,
dupe a nation abundant in surplus buttons?

Monsieur Verdoux

Man, you're only as old
as the women you feel.
With three failed marriages –
the third a drunk
who attempted blackmail
then went to court
to get him jailed –
Charlie Chaplin
thought he was thoroughly through
with thespian women.

He was plotting the murders
of Monsieur Verdoux
when he first set eyes
on Oona O'Neill –
almond-eyed, demure,
just seventeen.
Chaplin was fifty-seven.

Ignoring the sneers,
they went at it
like rabbits
until, thirty years
and eight kids later,
Charlie called it a day
and went to Heaven.

Witchfinder General

What shall you know of pure love
now that passion has passed out
with hot pants, ski pants,
and, Lord God, leg-warmers?
What shall you know of the difficulties
to overcome, when such misuse
fashions the people?

City, what shall become of us
because of you?
Who shall be uncontaminated,
who shall desire love purely
unsolicited,
where shall love flourish
untempted,
in what malignant place shall I find it?

The Last Picture Show

What happened downtown to your American hope
when your hair was long and you were younger.
Who bought you drinks in lush hotels
and brought you down to low motels.
How did your affair with Big Shot begin,
was he cold or hot and were you
good to him in the desert of his prairie bed.
Driving alone to the picture show,
did anyone watch you go?

In the burning blues of big towns, California,
with its totems and wagons with jet fighter fins,
were you just a shadow at sundown,
a silhouette on an uptown screen,
ash at the end of a king-size cigarette.
Did you think it would come to an end,
did you hope it would turn out to be true,
did you leave before the end of the show.
In the end was there anyone
at all to see you go?

What happened downtown to your American hope
when you were young and your hair was longer.

14. From **SPIRIT OF BRADFORD**

Out of Passion with the Times

Feet planted apart on a pedestal,
a hand half-raised, warning perhaps
of the storm from the East
blowing back the tails of his topcoat.
A Bulldog Drummond aspect in the face,
the dogged stance of Churchill.
Flanked by the theatre and library,
centre-stage on a low green hill;
at night lit up for posterity.

They turned your back
on the National Museum of Photography
Film and Television,
as though in apology for the age
which got shot of Swan Arcade,
built when alpaca from Peru
and angora from Asia Minor
made Bradford what it was:
wool capital with an empire.
You never forgave the disgrace,
a thunderous frown rumbles,
your jowls quiver as you contemplate
the improvements of Wardley:
the motorway and muggers' subway
epitomise that cocky epoch
of Billy Liar
and Room at the Top.

JB, look down from your pedestal:
the city you see
is not the city you saw
from your clerk's window
before the '14-'18 War
buried the dream of love,
good companions and camaraderie,
and turned dead men into memorials.

Shelled in 1894, the year after
Keir Hardie and G.B. Shaw
banged the soles of the feet
of the Independent Labour Party
near a cinema in Peckover Street.
The Bradford of Jack the Lad
was a place of hard corners,
a city of dirt and grandeur:
sooty murk and acrid smells
resounding with the racket of money,
Bands of Hope and glorious Messiahs.
A place of sheep and goats,
chapels and hills, valleys and mills,
where yarns were spun
and threads were woven
into shimmering cloth and thick-skinned coats.

In 1911 you were sixteen
when City won the FA Cup.
Thousands crammed Market Street,
eager for broadsheet pages
packed with eight point;
each paragraph as long
as a chapter in a modern novel.
Yet we are supposed to believe
common men could barely write or read.
On the contrary they were hungry then,
and read the news with relish.

Look down in vain for W.E. Forster,
he does not stand where he used to be.
Cast away on a traffic island,
surrounded by a round-about,
a hand half-raised above
the love-wrecked
bus inspector's shed.
In the new iron age when money's rule
measured men like lengths of cloth
and only those as tall as money
could afford the fees for school -
the others were taught to doff -
Forster took up the fight.

He forced Parliament to concede
that even ragged-arsed half-timers
should learn to read and write.
In vain look down for Richard Oastler,
Nonconformist and abolitionist.
Repulsed by the slavery in Bradford's mills
where quick-limbed nippers weekly
worked sixty to seventy hours
for coppers, rickets, rheumatic chills,
Oastler fought for twenty years despite
the loss of friends and health.
His conscience, offended by his sight,
rebelled against the poverty of Godless wealth.
Dickens was writing Oliver Twist
when furious Oastler tried to enlist
Wellington for the Ten Hours Bill.
The Iron Duke was not for turning,
a phrase that echoes still.

Look down at Centenary Square:
you will not see Sir Titus there.
Considered a hindrance to motor traffic,
Salt was removed and now erodes
in Lister Park, his face towards Saltaire.
He could have built a mansion on a hill
or retired to the South of France.
Instead Salt pursued his vision:
a palace of industry -
golden stone and reflective glass -
built upon the waters of the Aire.
He used the profits of his cloth
to build strong homes of stone and brick;
a hospital, church and school;
a library twelve hundred volumes thick.
Life, to be of moral worth,
meant good works and work well-wrought:
Sir Titus sought a social fabric.

Salt was a Morley man:
Huddersfield bred Oastler:
Forster a Dorsetshire Quaker -
outsiders to a man. Unlike you JB,
they fought this place of hard corners.

You chose to leave to make your mark
on the city where you began:
you left before it broke your heart.

Up there on your pedestal,
imposing but somehow ridiculous.
What do the young make of you?
Old fart in a flasher's mac,
head spattered by bird-shit,
privates spray-painted white -
the handiwork of a modern wit.
Little Germany and World's End
echo faintly with forgotten Messiahs.
The young do not care for men
posturing on pedestals;
nor would you want them to,
remembering idolatry's poverty
and what it fed in the Thirties.
Crumpled cans and empty pop
bottles shoved in municipal
flowerbeds at your feet -
these are their memorials,
lit up at night for posterity.

Where is Billy Liar
now falsehood is commonplace
and truth is made up for a lark?
Where is Billy Liar now
there is no escape to London
and Joe Lampton bleeds alone in the dark?
A courthouse has replaced the station,
Billy Liar makes believe to deceive the truth,
Charlie Chaplin mourns Jimmy the Fearless,
the lost Empire of his built-on youth.
Lights go up in The Playhouse
where Simone Signoret
lights yet another cigarette
and cries alone for Joe Lampton.
Lost in darkness. While another voice,
a different messiah, ghetto-blasts
the plaintive past.

We don't drink cocktails:
our Molotovs come from Gaza.
We torch their four-door
saloon showrooms the better
to magnify our silhouettes.
Intifada fatwa warning
black and red and green
writing on walls of mills and churches.
The curved blade of our faith
flashes in the fires we set.

Mohammed's moon rises
above the mosque's bronze dome,
an axe at twilight.
My Monte Cristo windows
frame cold midnight:
the police helicopter's zone.
Over all our heads
the moonlit chopper hovers.

Man's estate goes under Rabys hammer.
Smelling of loneliness and mothballs,
cherished furniture of spinsters and widows
in St Catherine's dead or waiting to die.
We shouldn't attach our feelings
to weather or coincidence, but we do;
deciding the day is unpropitious,
as though rain on high windows
somehow makes a difference.

No sound of the bells on Sunday
but the muezzin,
curling up to Heaven
like smoke from lamb.
And in summer
ice cream vans thrice daily
bring Match of the Day,
and the Good, the Bad and the Ugly.

Now Bradford echoes with another voice
should we rejoice JB?
Dead men are fit for memorials
when what they did when living
is out of passion with the times –
its kick-boxing princes in blousons,
LA bomber jackets, baseball caps,
hoods, headscarves and 501s,
chador-black hair sharked back.

Like Salt and Forster and Oastler
you were not wrought by fashion,
but fashioned by what you thought and felt.
You stand now as you stood then:
for love, good companions, camaraderie.
Though disfigured and slowly eroding,
adorned with laurels of graffiti,
neglected but not forgotten.

Four For David Hockney

I. 1954 Self Portrait

Strange bird in a gilded cage,
staring uncertainly at the world
beyond a fringe.
Perry Como and Princess Margaret
were all the rage
when I pushed a pram about Bradford's streets,
my dolls fat silver piglets of paint.
Artists were respected
only if they looked like something else,
so I affected
the clothes of an accountant.
T.S. Eliot, William Burroughs, René Magritte
dressed like that in the Fifties.
In all that pinstripe get-up
I looked like a lesbian librarian
disguised as Peter Sellers.
You had to keep the bastards guessing.

II. Portrait of the Artist's Old Man

My father never liked the look of doors;
he emulsioned ochre sunsets on ours.
Clerking most of his working life,
he painted posters for cinemas
and signs for shops that wanted them.
He peddled recycled bicycles, and
wheeled an armchair to the corner call-box.
Ideas like that came naturally,
besides, we were a family of seven.
Things dad did looked dotty only to folk
who couldn't see the wonder, logic, or necessity.

III. Abracadaver – It's Only Me

I learned more about life
                    painting
in the dead room of the Infirmary
than in the studios of the Royal College.
They didn't know what to make of me:
Northern working class but evidently queer,
John Ogdon glasses, gold jacket and golden hair.
Watch them eyeing the Dog Paintings now,
wondering privately if deaf Hockney –
miniature hair-driers in each ear –
is barking or laughing at them.
Some people like to be offended:
I learned that in my very first year.

IV. It Makes No Difference

Forgive me for dyeing my hair
blond and finding the world beautiful
which, to you, is ugly and unfair.
Forgive me for being lucky.

Forgive me for not measuring success
by another's failure. I never expected
to fail, nor waited for doors to open.
Forgive me for making money.

Forgive me for living in Hollywood
where no one dwells in retrospect
and even the colours are rich –
and the weather is not introspective.

Forgive me for not seeking revenge
to shame an ungrateful or indifferent
world. It was never that to me.
Forgive me, though it makes no difference.

15. THE BOTTOM LINE

Message in a Bottle: To Wendy Cope who wrote *Making Cocoa For Kingsley Amis*.

Coping with Wendy's nightly cocoa
must have made Kingsley Amis retch.
I once went to the house he shared
with wife Number One (he lived upstairs).
There were ten green bottles on the step,
all empty. The old devil's idea
of a nightcap was a draught of vintage,
cooled and bottled in Provence.

That Welsh no-good boyo, who chose to burn
his green fuse to the bitter end,
might have lived longer under Milk Wood
as a milky chocoholic; but Wendy,
in cocoa veritas sounds neither right nor good.
I raise my glass and offer this thought:
we're all at sea, *waving or drowning,*
but in a tempest one usually hopes for port.

The Bottom Line – for Jonathan Silver

These days the only thing that counts
some say, is the bottom line –
preceded by the dollar sign's treble clef.
Only large amounts make the right kind of music,
the rest is just conversation. The only time
black is beautiful is when we're in it.

The road between us is divided by lines,
flashing by like cats' eyes or minus signs.
Red lights lead to her secret heart,
yellow ones to mine.
Though I know she would rather
lullaby lambs with hymns
on the threadbare bedspread of a Pennine hillside
than exchange words with me,
still she fills the room like the smell of oregano,
the reddest of love's red wine.

Love, there's no accounting for it:
things don't always add up on the bottom line.

I sometimes think God only reveals Himself
in places you least expect to find.
How else explain my peculiar rapture
when rain hits the windows
of the backstreet launderette
where I watch my washing
orbit the bathysphere
Speed Queen Drying Tumbler
manufactured in Brooklyn.

As though responding to the earth's need
rain slants irregularly in lines,
pauses, then intensifies its lovemaking.
Perhaps it's my age or a sign of the times,
but my eyes are distracted continually
by lovely undulating lines.
There's no way to describe, no words to define
the curve of her eyebrows, her lips,
the arc of the earth spinning through time,
without love or poetry.
Surreptitiously these things undermine
my attempts to think straight on the bottom line.

Some say we are digits,
balancing like circus midgets
on the tightrope of the bottom line.
Mine sags as I get older;
yet within the sadder shape I make
my eyes still see the outline
of something taut, heroic, fine.
I do not deny it. *Signore, ascolta!*
Puccini still makes me cry
at sunset. Across the valley,
streetlights are the keys of a saxophone.
They remind me.

Screw love, some say, make money.
But the wind's sound making the copper beech
count reminds me of the sea,
not greenbacks in a Swiss account.

Love like poetry offers another opportunity
to change the rhythm or alter the rhyme.
In poetry you almost always find
the bottom line the least satisfactory.

Ten Poems for Jonathan

In the Beginning

God fashioned the cloths of heaven
and, sometime after lunch a ball of clay.
On Tuesday He split the atom
and divided night from day.
Anticipating the need for loaves and fishes,
on Wednesday He made continents and oceans.

Missing something, though what God did not know,
He imagined trains, boats,
Virgin Atlantic, and even cars.
Come Thursday God, still bemused,
killed a million millennia or two
mass-producing suns and moons and stars.

Fish swam into His brain, on Friday of course;
snakes in the grass, animals, mammals
and assorted birds of prey.
After five days He was jiggered,
so on Saturday God created Jonathan –
who immediately opened the place on Sunday.

The Impossibility of the Idea of Art in the Mind of Someone Hungry

It was sacrilege, wolfing the shepherd's pie
darling David had concocted high
in Hollywood's million dollar hills.
He would have framed it, or borne it
lovingly back to teeth-picking Bradford,
home of West Yorkshire's famous pies.

A Hockney original by a bottle
of Croft, between the Rake's Progress
and Burmantoft. Imagine the spread
Paris Match would have commissioned:
nouvelle cuisine de l'anglais d'Eccleshill.
Hockney's new direction

might have embarked demon Damien
on a course of art more digestible
than a shark in embalming fluid.
Sharks should be eaten, not displayed
at the Tate. But David's pie proved irresistible
to hungry Jonathan, who could not wait.

Yorkshire's Great Deli-Llama

Where pelts from Peruvian Alpacas
were once sorted, washed or woven,
he sat making menus
for his New York-style Diner.
Yorkshire's great deli-llama
climbed more mountains than Julie Andrews.

Burning up time and life's
long and winding road,
he slid down rainbows
by the seat of his pants.
He smashed through the roof
and blew open the world's picture windows.

Nodding off nightly before
Trevor McDonald or Michael Buerk
got to work on the nation's nerves,
he rose with the larks.
He relished work which love
turned into energy and preserves.

The Man Who Laughed at Wisdom

Where others saw only contradiction
his Phoenician eyes configured
symmetry, unspotted opportunities.
Reflecting his view of life his studio-
cum-office juxtaposed junk and treasures:
a mixture of Matisse and Steptoe.

Like the Magi gambling on Bethlehem,
he hoped for the unexpected.
Like an astronaut he walked in space
and saw what it might become.
A master converter, an unshaven Spinoza,
who embraced Götterdämmerung

and laughed at Norman Wisdom.
I never saw him leer at smut,
trade in bullshit or give out crap.
Brusque, bemusing, sometimes abrupt,
yet always he caused me to wonder.
Only gifted artists, I think, do that.

Intimations of Mortality

Appalled, I watched
him stoop to remove his shoes
and, laughing, slowly unpeel each sock.
Though late on Friday afternoon,
such ad hoc behaviour
startled. I confess I was shocked.

Worse followed.
One Saturday, after lunch thank God,
I watched my human dynamo –
tailing dachshunds in the Gallery –
almost tenderly scoop up poop
with a pan and brush.

Such intimations of mortality,
though innocuous enough,
often prove too much
for unwise idolaters whom
life perversely obliges
to live vicariously.

The Soldier

Yorkshire regiments in war
fight stubbornly. Though Yorkshire
born and bred and Bradford to the core,
five thousand years of history
helped him fight the invasion
of his body's borders; two years or more

against the alien enemy
he rallied every resisting guerrilla cell.
His friends were helpless allies;
unable to reinforce his innate
but depleted resources, they watched
his long refusal to capitulate.

The more malignant the disease
he, I swear, gazed at humanity
more benignly, as though he and death
shared some secret knowledge. In the arms
of his family he died as he lived,
without bitterness or regret.

The Third Man

After Roger died I was like Job,
hoping to be forgotten.
Then God sent death for Jonathan.
Auf wiedersehen: Goodnight
Vienna. Now, like Joseph Cotton,
I wonder where Harry Lime has gone.

His familiar parking spot is empty,
I no longer hope to see his dark green
Bentley. His shoes have gone for a walk,
he won't be back. My mornings wake me
to fog and loss, yet the weather
does not bite nor lash enough.

More than most he made a bigger splash;
his charisma still hangs in the air,
an aromatic and exotic essence.
I sense him everywhere;
the Third Man is always with me.
His absence is like a presence.

A Blue Cardigan

Thank you for forty-four tall windows,
the white columns, October's golden light.
Thank you for stripping the setts,
giving me acoustical stones to hear
my eager steps. All I wanted was a place
to root my rootless longing to belong.

At my customary place, table five,
back to the south-facing window,
Hockney's California-coloured visions
of Coxwold and Bridlington,
my customary cappuccino and Hamlet,
waiting for you to surprise me.

The telephone bleeps insistently,
but it is not you, ringing in
from your rose-garden, your gait
slowed but dignified by pain.
A blue cardigan catches my eye:
my heart rises and then dies again.

Strictly No Black Ties

Death certificates, the bureaucracy
of dying, the necessary accounting.
He hated formality: *strictly no
black ties*. He should have simply vanished,
vaporised by half-a-kilo of TNT,
focal point of an assassin's

trigonometry, like Gianni Versace.
Twenty-five days into September,
the middle of week thirty-nine,
two hundred and sixty-eight steps
into the last year they gave him,
his forty-eighth birthday

less than a mortal month away.
But long enough to celebrate
twenty-five years of married love,
Silver his anniversary.
Now beyond the job of solemn morticians,
wholly himself again in eternity.

Tulips

Grace is not an abstract idea:
it floats incarnately
over the face of the earth.
After thunder, after rain
the earth is blessed
with the smell of flowers.

The measure of a man is whether
he makes a difference.
After life, after death
fate floats invisibly.
Above the smell of the earth
substantiality seems hollow.

What brought us here
if not something tangible,
ineffable but clear?
After death, after life
it is the magic star
we cannot touch but follow.

Wetbacks in Heptonstall

Uphill all the way to the cemetery.
Thirty-nine steps above the roof

of The Fox and Goose, the gap in the valley
where the road comes in. A tube

in the uterus. Mytholmroyd, Sowerby:
gritstone names synonyms for migraine.

Shrugging muscle-bound shoulders,
winter's hills steam like sweating soldiers

marooned on manoeuvres in bandit country.
My road ends in a cloven hoof:

right to Blackshaw Head, left to the dead.
In an old church field

she has her last piece of real estate.
A rose with thorns grows above her heart;

but she cannot be scratched by mortality
with its human passions and art.

Like an old maid rocking on a veranda,
she gazes upward with amusement

at those who come to visit her
in the rain. Wetbacks at the border

of a familiar but foreign country
they dare not cross or enter.

Fibres

I do not often look at the roses
and the cream carnations of the carpet,
woven in the heavy woollen district,
on my bedroom floor.
They make me remember
the man who roomed next door
in college. A humble gardener
training to be a teacher.
He managed a boys football team
and proudly played Beethoven's Fifth
to annoy the friends who tormented him.
Scenting his loneliness keener than bloodhounds
a convict on the run, they taped over his door
with toilet-paper, and mocked his music
to provoke protestations
which incited more mirth.
A gardener, humbled by a vocation
greater than his gifts: a perennial victim.
They arrested him in winter
for killing a kid he'd picked up;
matching fibres from the body
with an off-cut in the boot
of his Morris 1800.
The flowers in my bedroom carpet
remind me of his silent months in college,
his loud symphony, his mortified friends
from whom he slyly kept his secret knowledge.

The Omagh Bombing and a Birthday

The afternoon was like any other somnolent Saturday
mid-August: marketing to be done, gossip
swapped, bets placed each way; a new season
about to kick-off, a special day
anticipated like the morning's frying bacon,
evening's hoped for assignation.

Les Misérables was halfway through the matinée
at home, United were one down
and I was half-asleep. Someone was kissing
you somewhere, this was your day,
your twenty-ninth year, my third without you,
Lucy's Day: sunny, white and blue.

The only decision for me to make
was what to cook and eat to remain awake
until time legitimised the hour when I might sleep.
I drank hot tea in the dark and listened,
smoked by the open window, batting flies away.
Hadn't they warned us on Good Friday?

The day was followed by another. I reconnected
the phone – no one had called to tell me their troubles.
The radio counted the dead: twenty-eight,
one for each of the years which had taken her
to twenty-nine, and put me twenty ahead.
I read Auden's lament for Yeats

and, drowning between sleep and awake,
believed my mother was still alive.
I woke not knowing where I was, dazed,
wanting touch, my hair wet. And I thought
how the days flash by without a sound,
and how like coffins the years go down.

August 15, 1998